ETHICS, ECONOMICS AND POLITICS

Ethics, Economics and Politics

Principles of Public Policy

I. M. D. LITTLE

OXFORD
UNIVERSITY PRESS

OXFORD

Great Clarendon Street, Oxford OX2 6DP

Oxford University Press is a department of the University of Oxford.
It furthers the University's objective of excellence in research, scholarship,
and education by publishing worldwide in

Oxford New York

Auckland Bangkok Buenos Aires Cape Town Chennai
Dar es Salaam Delhi Hong Kong Istanbul Karachi Kolkata
Kuala Lumpur Madrid Melbourne Mexico City Mumbai Nairobi
São Paulo Shanghai Taipei Tokyo Toronto

Oxford is a registered trade mark of Oxford University Press
in the UK and in certain other countries

Published in the United States
by Oxford University Press Inc., New York

The moral rights of the author have been asserted
Database right Oxford University Press (maker)

First published 2002
Published in paperback 2003

All rights reserved. No part of this publication may be reproduced,
stored in a retrieval system, or transmitted, in any form or by any means,
without the prior permission in writing of Oxford University Press,
or as expressly permitted by law, or under terms agreed with the appropriate
reprographics rights organization. Enquiries concerning reproduction
outside the scope of the above should be sent to the Rights Department,
Oxford University Press, at the address above

You must not circulate this book in any other binding or cover
and you must impose this same condition on any acquirer

Little, Ian Malcolm David.
Ethics, economics, and politics : principles of public policy / I.M.D. Little.
p. cm.
Includes bibliographical references
1. Economics – Philosophy.   2. Economics – Moral and ethical aspects.
3. Political science—Philosophy. I. Title.
HB72 .L575 2002   320'.6'01–dc21   2002072440

ISBN 0–19–925704–3 (hbk)
ISBN 0–19–926872–X (pbk)

1 3 5 7 9 10 8 6 4 2

Typeset by Newgen Imaging Systems (P) Ltd., Chennai, India
Printed in Great Britain
on acid-free paper by
Biddles Ltd., Guildford and King's Lynn

Contents

Preface and Acknowledgements

I began to plan this book on 18th December, 1998, my 80th birthday. However, because of illness not much was done until the new millenium began. It was submitted to Oxford University Press on 9th August 2001. As the reader will discover, the book is more about moral and political philosophy than anything else. With very few exceptions, as an active economist, I had not read any philosophy for 50 years. The exceptions included books by John Rawls, 1971, Robert Nozick, 1974, and Anthony de Jasay, 1985. During this time there has been a lot written of relevance to the present book. I have not read more than a small fraction of it: but enough, I hope, to point some students in the right direction for further study.

The more recent philosophers who have most influenced me have been John Broome, Anthony de Jasay, and Robert Sugden, as the references to their work will testify. It is interesting that all three began as economists (and Robert Sugden is still a professor of economics).

The following have read and commented on the whole book: Wilfred Beckerman, Vijay Joshi, Anthony Quinton, and Robert Skidelsky. Others who have read part of it include: Ken Binmore, John Broome, Anthony de Jasay, Robert Sugden, and Peter Oppenheimer. Tim Besley also gave some advice on political economy. They have saved me from some errors and infelicities, but I have not always accepted their suggestions. I am grateful to all of these but the usual disclaimers apply. I am especially grateful to Peter Oppenheimer without whose late intervention this book might never have appeared.

Finally, I am most deeply indebted to my wife, Lydia, who has typed and retyped the whole book, taking time off from her more artistic work as a sculptor. Her computer skills have occasionally been supported by those of my stepson, Joseph Lenthall.

Introduction

This book studies the three interfaces of ethics, economics, and politics. Any well-considered view of the most desirable role for the State in various aspects of our lives implies some serious thinking about these subjects, and the way in which they interact. This can be done without academic training in any of them. Therefore, this book is intended to inform not only students but also any person with an interest in public affairs.

I believe that many universities now have joint schools including at least two of the three subjects. A few have a school comprising all three, including Yale and Oxford. Oxford has long had a school known as PPE (philosophy, politics, and economics), but the teaching and exams have not been planned to emphasize the relationship of the subjects to each other. A more integrated school would always have been possible, but I believe that recent thinking in these subjects, in the past 25 years, has made this interdisciplinary possibility more exciting.

Each of our subjects can be divided into branches. Some of these branches of any one subject are closely related to other subjects, others less so or hardly at all. Let us glance at our subjects with this in mind. The branches of philosophy that will almost exclusively concern us are moral and political philosophy. We shall be discussing their relationship to politics and economics at length. However, if we confine ourselves to these branches what have we left out, and can we justify this neglect?

The other most important branches of philosophy are epistemology and logic. These are concerned with knowledge, truth, and meaning. In some sense every branch of knowledge, every science, presupposes that knowledge can be acquired, that propositions can be true or false, and sentences understood. But there is no special relation to economics or politics. We shall not be concerned with epistemology or logic because they are too profound. These apart, almost every field of enquiry generates books and articles entitled *The Philosophy of* ——, where the blank may stand for history, law, mathematics, religion, the physical, and social sciences, and indeed economics. These philosophies are concerned with the concepts, methodology, and the explicit or implicit assumptions of

the designated subject. Economics apart, they are mainly periph-
eral to our central interests, and we shall not need to explore them.
This may seem puzzling in the case of the sciences, especially the
social sciences, since economics is after all a social science.

Before resolving the puzzle it is useful to try to define economics
itself, and then to make a distinction between positive and normative economics. Economics is part of sociology if the latter is
defined as the study of individual persons, and groups of persons,
interacting in society. This study includes what benefits and harms
such persons or groups. In other words, it is concerned with their
welfare.

How do we separate economics from other branches of sociology?
A.C. Pigou had an answer in *The Economics of Welfare* that has been
widely accepted. He wrote 'The one obvious instrument of measurement available in social life is money. Hence, the range of our
enquiry becomes restricted to that part of social welfare that can be
brought directly or indirectly into relation with the measuring rod
of money'.[1] This definition is imperfect. First, economists study
relationships where the rewards or incentives need not be
expressed in monetary terms. Second, and more important, what
can legitimately be brought into line with the measuring rod of
money is debatable. The value of life is the most awesome example.
But while there are these problems with the definition it is, I think,
good enough to be going along with.

Positive economics is concerned to measure economic facts
and relationships, and to produce causal explanations of economic
events and trends. Normative economics is concerned with whether
one economic state of affairs is better or worse than another, and
hence with the question whether one action or measure, one policy
or institutional framework, is better than another in the light of its
probable consequences. It is, thus, essentially teleological. Normative economic problems range from whether or not to widen some
road, through whether to fix the foreign exchange rate, to the design
of economic decision-making institutions and procedures.

Closely related to the positive/normative distinction is that
between descriptive statements on the one hand, and prescriptive
statements or value judgements on the other. This latter is a much-
discussed distinction that we shall consider at length later in the
book. A preliminary view follows.

---

[1] A.C. Pigou *The Economics of Welfare*, fourth edition 1946, p. 11.

Suppose that I say 'Smith has a better life than Jones'. If someone challenges this, I will normally produce facts that most people would consider to be relevant, such as Smith has a high salary and is physically very fit, while Jones is handicapped and less well paid. But such facts are contestable, and even if agreed are not conclusive. No elaboration of similar facts is conclusive either, for there are no generally agreed criteria for scaling a person's well-being. Such judgements cannot be definitely verified or falsified, and for this reason are commonly thought to be unscientific.

A fortiori, this is true of judgements about the welfare of different groups of people, or the same group at different times. However, such judgements are of direct concern for, or even determine, economic recommendations and decisions. They are therefore best considered to be value judgements and to belong to normative rather than positive economics. The same is true of many economic judgements that do not obviously proclaim their ethical nature by the use of words such as welfare or well-being. Judgements of economic efficiency are of this type because economic efficiency is ultimately a function of the rate of transformation of scarce resources into welfare.

Similarly, like most boundaries, that between positive and normative is not precise. Take inflation. Economists may agree the precise measure—the rate of increase of some index of prices—and try to measure the effect of various causes on this measure. Equally positively they may recognize some other measure, and use that in their calculations. But something called the rate of inflation is of importance to non-professionals, for instance to voters. When a politician thunders that some policy would be inflationary he is clearly condemning it. Economics shares with other social sciences the fact that its findings are often relevant to policy. Great care has to be taken by a social scientist who wants to preserve his or her scientific status that findings are not taken as recommendations if this is not intended. The findings should not use persuasive language. Of course, the economist or other social scientist may passionately want to be influential. In that case he or she may be happy to abandon scientific integrity.

Much of the work of most economists is positive, or scientific. This includes description of the many components of economic states of affairs, and predictions of their future values; the building of analytic models to illustrate or help solve economic problems;

and in general the measurement of economic relations. This positive work gives rise to conceptual and methodological problems which are common to all sciences. The social sciences differ from the natural or physical sciences mainly because the behaviour of the variables, and their relationships, is less constant.

The philosophy of science is, almost by definition, concerned with the discovery and truth of positive laws or relationships. Positive economics is not essentially different from other sciences. However, we in this book are interested in the interface of normative economics with moral and political philosophy, which is why we said earlier that we would not be concerned with the philosophy of science.

We turn to politics. Politics is mainly about the solution of problems of coordination by authority rather than by the market or by spontaneous agreement. Since all such solutions affect the distribution of wealth and welfare, politics is also inevitably concerned with distribution. At the theoretical level whether some problem of coordination has a spontaneous solution, or equilibrium, and whether it is a good solution, is studied by the relatively new and still exploding discipline of game theory.[2] We shall have occasion to refer to this theory again in Parts II and III, for it is a major component of the interfaces of both philosophy and economics, and philosophy and politics.

The delivery of commodities to the point of sale, and their purchase by consumers, seems to be a miracle of coordination of a great many independent individual decisions. Of course, it is true that good market coordination depends on laws, conventions, and financial institutions. Their substance and formation are the subject of politics, but the actual production and market transactions are not political.

The supply and enjoyment of some commodities and services is not left to individual production and exchange, either because the latter could not supply the goods in question or is not trusted to do so. This arises mostly when the good or service is large and indivisible and therefore cannot be sold in small units. National defence is the prime example. In other cases public production or distribution, or both, may be undertaken only because the government decides that the outcome would be better than if left to private initiative. In these cases, production and distribution has

---

[2] So named after the seminal work, von Neumann and Morgenstern, *The Theory of Games and Economic Behavior*.

become a political activity. However, private activities may also be so regulated that authority plays a major role in determining the production and distribution of goods and services.

Our definition of political activity does not limit it to governmental activity, whether national, municipal, or local. A private road may serve the interests of several households. If they are very few the problem of who pays how much for its maintenance may be resolved by unstructured agreement. But if there are rather more households orderly reconciliation of their differing interests my require the creation of some decision-making procedures, and some authority to implement decisions. The same applies to a variety of private institutions such as colleges, clubs, and trade unions. Politics includes the study of their governments.

It may be objected that our definition of politics is too broad. A family has problems of coordination and these are not resolved by any internal market. Are we then to say that family decisions are essentially political? Why not? However, in practice few students of politics study intra-family relationships, and we shall not concern ourselves with them despite the fact that governments pass laws that influence them, for example, that parents may not smack children.

As in the case of economics, the subject of politics may be divided into positive and normative branches. Positive politics describes political institutions, decision-making procedures, and activities intended to change or influence them. It can be concerned with all levels of government, and with all its executive, legislative, and judicial branches. It studies the political behaviour of citizens, and the provenance and behaviour of politicians. It seeks to discover the causes of change in the laws and regulations of society. A central issue is, of course, how governments are formed and possibly removed. It is a vast subject that can range over all the countries of the world and most of history.

There is an interface between positive politics and economics. Governments affect the workings of an economy in many ways: they raise taxes, make laws, pass decrees, and so regulate the behaviour of producers and consumers alike. The nature and thrust of these influences vary with the kind of regime or state of which the government is part. This variety may stem from different beliefs about the workings of the economy. For instance, whatever the aims of government, the degree of belief in the efficacy of planning versus laisser-faire clearly varies: here ideology may play as large a part as dispassionate reasoning and economic research. However, the aims of governments also vary. Economists have naively tended to assume that all governments embrace individualistic values, and are solely concerned to maximize the welfare of the people. But more communitarian values have been apparent in many countries, for instance a strong state, independence, national pride, and even rising numbers. One must also recognize that the dominant aim of politicians and rulers is often their own enrichment, including that of their families and friends. This has been common throughout history.

The study of these ideologies and aims is part of positive politics, although what is desirable may be of passionate concern to rulers, subjects, and even external observers. This makes dispassionate study difficult but not impossible. The relative economic success (measured in various dimensions) of governments of varying degrees of autocracy and democracy, of liberality and repression, can be and is indeed also studied.

Citizens do not always take their government's law, taxes and regulations, as given. They lobby either individually or in 'interest groups' for changes beneficial to themselves. They also bribe politicians and civil servants. Economists now call these activities 'rent-seeking'. The more far-reaching and detailed a government's influence and control is, the greater the room for rent-seeking activity. Corruption has in most countries become a major problem, which it is important but very difficult to study.

It is also clear that economic performance as judged by the citizens, or certain groups of citizens, may react on government; it influences voters, if votes there are. Even in very autocratic regimes, the mass of the people usually has some influence. In certain circumstances, particular unpopular measures—such as changes in taxation—can unseat governments.

These interfaces of politics and economics are too numerous and varied for us to be able to deal with them all. We shall concentrate on those that throw most light on the question of how extensive we would like government to be.

We have attempted rough definitions of economics and politics. We shall end this introduction with a rough definition of moral and political philosophy. First, we maintain that political philosophy is a branch of moral philosophy. Its primary concern is with the problems of (1) whether a citizen has a duty or an obligation to obey the state, and (2) with the corresponding problem of the legitimacy of a state, or, in other words, what right a state has to coerce its subjects. The very language we have used to describe these concerns of political philosophy proclaims that they are moral problems and that therefore political philosophy is a branch of moral philosophy.

What then is moral philosophy? I shall here embrace the cliché that a subject may be defined by what its practitioners do. Some moral philosophers mainly analyse moral concepts and their logical structure, and the uses of prescriptive language. Such language has a certain logic of its own which differs from that of descriptive analysis. For instance, it is not a strict contradiction to say both 'do it' and 'it is not the right thing to do': but there is a tension which cries out for explanation. The most original and influential work of this type is that of R.M. Hare, followed by many others including himself.[3] It is sometimes called meta-ethics.

Other moral philosophers try to find a set of principles which will systematize what ordinary people believe to be right actions, or good states of affairs; or they pull to pieces other philosophers' attempts to formulate such a synthesis. This is because the synthesizers often appeal to consensus, and their opponents shoot them down by producing examples or dilemmas where the principles would lead to results that, it is claimed, would confound the deepest intuitions of many people. In the end they appeal to what is 'plausible' or 'acceptable', or what seems to amount to the same thing, the intuitions of common sense. At the same time they usually declare their hostility to intuitionism, for the good reason that, whatever their epistemological basis is supposed to be, people's moral intuitions conflict, and quite often even a single person's intuitions may conflict with each other.

But some sort of reconciliation can perhaps be produced, provided that too much is not claimed. If a theory, or set of principles, does not run counter to a few of the most deeply felt intuitions of most people, then it may help them to sort out any inconsistency in their moral views, and even help them in situations when they are not sure what they ought to do. Perhaps different moral theories

---

[3] R.M.Hare, *The Language of Morals*, 1952. In the preface he writes 'Ethics, as I conceive it, is the logical study of the language of morals'. See also Hare (1981, 1989).

may themselves be judged in terms of their value in these respects; and the same person may even find different moral theories helpful in different circumstances. What is surely unobtainable is a moral theory that applies universally. More than two thousand years of failure to find one supports this view.

Finally, some philosphers try to show that there are deeper reasons than intuition or self-interest why we should obey certain moral rules. Of course, for the great majority of people over most of historical time, moral rules were to be obeyed because they were the dictates of God, or the gods. But in western societies since the Enlightenment, beginning in the late seventeenth century, some philosophers have tried to show that certain principles can be derived from pure reason, or from the nature of man: the most famous and influential is Kant who proposed the principle of universalization, which states that one should always act in such a way that one can will that everyone should do the same in the same circumstances.[4] A corollary is that one should never treat another person merely as a means. These principles comprised the 'categorical imperative' which was advanced as a synthetic a priori truth—that is, a necessary metaphysical proposition which few if any modern empiricists would accept. However, the principle of universalization is itself widely accepted, and has been very influential.

[4] See *A Critique of Practical Reason*, 1788, or *Groundwork of the Metaphysic of Morals*, trs. H. Paton (1964).

PART I

ECONOMICS AND PHILOSOPHY

1

Personal Utility and Welfare

For 200 years the concept of utility has been thought of as a cornerstone of economics. The father of Utilitarianism, Jeremy Bentham, meant by utility whatever was conducive to happiness, which was a balance of pleasure and pain. Later, in recognition of the fact that what people wanted and would offer money for, was not always what would make them happy, utility came to mean desiredness. Later still, some 50 years ago, the meaning was further purged of psychological reference: if someone always chose A rather than B, economists said that this revealed a preference for A. Even this was not cleanly accurate and positive enough for some. People do not always choose what they prefer. It makes good sense to say 'I preferred B but chose A because my friends thought B was old fashioned' or even 'I preferred B but chose A because I thought it was better for me'. So finally, the meaning of utility came to be derived solely from choice. (But despite the above slightly pernickety argument utility is still often said to represent preferences.)

Utility theory requires that a person's economic choices are structured in the following way. The economic man or woman is supposed to choose from a large set of bundles consisting of quantities of various items. For every pair of bundles it is supposed that he or she would choose one or the other. Choices must be reflexive: if bundle A is chosen rather than B, then B must not be chosen rather than A. Choices must also be transitive: if A is chosen rather than B, and B rather than C, then A must be chosen rather than C. Together these two axioms define what is meant by consistency of choice. Given this consistency, a number can be attached to each bundle such that a bundle with a higher number is chosen rather than any one with a lower number. This is what is meant by a utility function, and by maximizing utility.[1]

---

[1] There is a tiresome mathematical complication in that there could be more bundles than numbers. In that event iso-utility, or indifference, has to be introduced if

The numbers referred to above are ordinal, which means that any
chosen set of numbers can be replaced by another set which pre-
serves the same order. Thus 1, 2, 3 can be replaced by, say, 17, 43, 101.
This implies that the differences have no significance. We can say
that A is greater than B, and B greater than C: but we cannot compare the difference between A and B with that between B and C.
More simply we cannot say, for instance, that the utility of A is
much greater than that of B. Such functions represent ordinal utility.

EXPECTED UTILITY AND RISK

Thus far the choice has been between certainties. If one opts for
bundle A one gets the the stated quantities of the different items.
But many economic choices involve uncertainty. One may be choosing between 'prospects' where the prospect is of getting one bundle
out of a set of bundles, each bundle having a certain probability of
being the one that one gets. To make a reasoned choice between
prospects it is not enough to be able to order bundles; one needs to
know not only the probabilities but also how much better one
bundle is than another.

Expected utility handles the choice between uncertain prospects.
The differences between the utility numbers become significant.
How is this done? To quote a famous source: 'Consider three events,
C, A, B, for which the order of the individual's preferences is the one
stated. Let p be a real number between 0 and 1 such that A is exactly
equally desirable with the combined event consisting of a chance of
probablility $1-p$ for B and the remaining chance of probability p for
C. Then we suggest the use of p as a numerical estimate for the ratio
of the preference of A over B to that of C over B'.[2]

mathematical continuity is to be preserved. The loss of introducing iso-utility is
that 'chosen rather than' no longer implies higher utility. This is the problem of
Buridan's ass which starved to death when equidistant from two equally attractive
bales of hay. The more sensible human would choose one rather than the other,
despite their iso-utility. The gain from iso-utility, or indifference as it is commonly
called, is that some circumlocution can be avoided. We shall ourselves later use indifference for this reason. Further discussion of all this can be found in I.M.D. Little,
A Critique of Welfare Economics (second edition, 1957, ch. 2 and Appendix 2).

[2] Von Neumann and Morgenstern, *The Theory of Games and Economic Behavior*,
p. 18 (I have substituted p for a). The original source of this method of cardinaliz-
ing utility is F.P. Ramsey, 'Truth and Probability' (1926) in *The Foundations of
Mathematics* (1931).

A numerical example may help. Suppose $p = 2/5$. Our U numbers must satisfy the relation: $U(A) = 3/5\,U(B) + 2/5\,U(C)$.

$U(A) = 70$; $U(B) = 50$; $U(C) = 100$ would do. The utility of A equals the expected utility of (B or C). But the numbers 140, 100, 200 or 240, 200, 300 would do as well. The utility function has been defined up to a linear transformation. This is called cardinal utility.

More generally, an expected utility function is written:

$$U(x_1, x_2, \ldots, x_n) = p_1\,U(x_1) + p_2U(x_2) + \ldots + p_nU(x_n).$$

In words, the utility of a prospect equals the sum of the utilities of the outcomes comprising the prospect each multiplied by the probability of its occurrence. Such a function is called 'additively separable'. The requirement for this is that the utility of any particular outcome is independent of all others. This is an important feature of a cardinal utility system. In our example, with the chosen numbers, A was indifferent to the prospect (B or C). This would be the case if the chooser was risk neutral. If he was risk averse he might choose the certain outcome A even if the expected utility of (B or C) was greater (and vice versa if he enjoyed risk). This is ruled out in our example. If expected utility is maximized A is chosen only if its utility is greater than the expected utility of (B or C). A is not allowed to become relatively more valuable because (B) and (C) are combined in an uncertain prospect. The importance of additive separability, and risk aversion or enjoyment are further discussed in the following sections.

RISK AND FLUCTUATIONS

The expected utility of the prospect of £100 or nothing depending on the toss of a coin, is equal to the expected utility of the prospect of £50 whichever way the coin falls. Anyone who is risk averse will, however, choose the sure thing of £50.

If we introduce the dimension of time, aversion to risk may come to much the same thing as aversion to a fluctuating income. Consider a college's investment policy over two periods, each of five years, one of which will be a bull market and the other a bear market. Initially it is a fifty-fifty chance as to whether it is a bull market or a bear market, but it is certain that bulls succeed bears and vice versa. The college can invest in gilts which give a moderate

Table 1.1.

		States of Nature			
		Bear	**Bull**	**Bear**	**Bull**
Periods	1	1	1	−1	4
	2	1	1	4	−1
Choice		**Gilts**		**Equities**	

certain income or equities which can fluctuate severely but which are sure to yield more than gilts over the long period. The choices (gilts and equities) are illustrated in Table 1.1.

The cells represent annual real income (in £m inclusive of capital gains and losses). Looking at the matter period by period the college is faced by the problem of risk, a certainty of £1m versus an expectation of £1.5m. Looking at the matter by states of nature there is a choice between a steady income of £1m and one fluctuating between an annual loss of £1m and a gain of £4m. With equities the period of loss could be very embarrassing, no research fellows and poor meals. But over the 10-year period the income is £15m against £10m with gilts. Over 50 years the college is either in the doldrums, or is an envied centre of learning.[3]

RISK AND EQUALITY

In the previous section, income prospects were considered in relation to states of nature (bull or bear markets) and to periods. They may also be considered in relation to states of nature, and to different persons as in Table 1.2, where the state of nature is determined by the toss of an unbiassed coin.

Suppose that you were invited to choose between the two hypothetical social systems, knowing only that you would be Person X or Person Y, but with absolutely no clue as to which. This is called choosing from behind 'a veil of ignorance'.[4]

[3] The example is obviously simplified and any relation to reality is more or less coincidental.

[4] This device of choosing from behind a veil of ignorance is due to John Harsanyi (1953). It was taken up and made famous by John Rawls (1971) and has been much debated. We shall come across it again. Obviously the example could be extended to

Table 1.2.

		States of Nature			
		Heads	Tails	Heads	Tails
Persons	X	2	2	1	10
	Y	2	2	10	1
Choice		Egalitarian system		Inegalitarian System	

Under egalitarianism you would get two units of income who-ever you were and whatever happened. Under inegalitarianism your income depends on who you turn out to be and which equiprobable state of nature occurs; but the upshot is that you have an equal chance of getting one unit or ten units (provided also that, having no clue as to whether you will be X or Y, you assume the chances are fifty–fifty). If you are very risk averse you would prob-ably choose egalitarianism. But your choice might well depend on absolute levels as well as comparative levels. For instance, if one unit of income was not too terrible to contemplate, I would choose inegalitarianism. This roughly corresponds to the idea of a safety net, and the view that one should care about absolute poverty (somehow defined), but that if everyone's basic needs (somehow defined) are satisfied then equality has no value. The case for inequality is strengthened when time is also brought into considera-tion, to the extent that greater incentives lead to faster growth. The value of equality, however, requires deeper discussion, and we revert to the subject in Chapter 6.

UTILITY AND POSITIVE ECONOMICS

I have said that utility was long regarded as a cornerstone of eco-nomics. But for positive economics utility theory, which is essent-ially a set of axioms defining consistency of choice, is almost valueless. Nothing follows from it, not even that people will buy less of something if its price, or relative price (that is, its opportunity

---

any number of persons, each with a probability of his being the chooser's incarna-tion, the probabilities summing to one. But two suffices to make the main point.

cost for the purchaser) rises. It may have some heuristic value, for instance in explaining the income and substitution effects of price changes; but that is all. Positive economists are certainly much concerned with demand, but with the aggregate demands of many persons. Thus most economists have no need to concern themselves with the rationality of choice of individuals. Admittedly, some study behaviour in small groups, even bilateral behaviour. Here some assumption about what governs behaviour is needed: but usually only that the participants try to win, or to maximize the monetary profits, pay-offs, or prizes, which are generated by the economic contests or games they play. A few economists even try to test utility theory: but that should perhaps count as psychology rather than economics.

UTILITY AND NORMATIVE ECONOMICS

However, utility theory really is a cornerstone of normative economics. Economists, and indeed all those concerned with policy, normally take greater utility to be a criterion of better-offness. If someone chooses situation A when he could have chosen B he is assumed to be better off in A than B. But a random choice does not imply a greater utility, which requires that the person's choices are consistent in the sense explained. So we should say that if someone is an economic man or woman and chooses A rather than B then he or she is better-off with A than with B.

A may be interpreted as a collection of goods and services, including savings, bought during some interval of time, say a year. B is any other collection he or she could have bought. In typical comparisons B is the collection bought in an earlier period (year 1). If our chooser's money income has risen, and prices are unchanged A is chosen and B could have been. If prices have changed one may value the quantities (q_{1s}) in collection B at the prices of year 2 (p_{2s}). $\Sigma p_2 q_2$ then represents expenditure on A, and $\Sigma p_2 q_1$ represents collection B revalued at the prices of year 2. If $\Sigma p_2 q_2 > \Sigma p_2 q_1$ it follows that B could have been chosen, and so A is chosen rather than B. In these circumstances it is said that the chooser's real income has risen.[5]

---

[5] I leave it to the reader to work out the meaning, if any, of the various other possible combinations of ps and qs.

It is easy to attack this criterion. First, economic man does not exist in any strict sense. People do not choose consistently. Much depends on the periods of observation. In short periods, less than a year, there is the problem of seasonality both in supply and in tastes. One is not really inconsistent in eating more ice cream in the summer, nor is one really worse-off because oysters are not available when there is no 'r' in the month. In short periods also, people may be apparently but not seriously inconsistent, because they want to experiment or like variety for its own sake. For long periods the difficulties are different but equally serious. People age and their tastes or circumstances change. One is not better-off if the price of tobacco falls if one has given up smoking but taken to champagne whose price has risen. One may have lost a leg or gone blind. One may have married or been divorced. Such changes and circumstances alter patterns of expenditure. The obvious importance of family matters may lead to the suggestion that a family should be regarded as the choosing unit; however, it takes but little thought to see that this introduces more problems than it solves.

Whatever the period under consideration, people make mistakes. They buy heroin, or they choose a career for which they are ill suited. It hardly needs saying that people do not always choose what is best for them. If one forces oneself to consider the very many reasons why it is wrong to say that an increase in someone's real income implies that he or she is better-off, one either dies of boredom or is almost bound to conclude that this criterion should be scuttled once and for all.

But driven to this logical conclusion one is forced to beat a hasty retreat.[6] Surely in most cases of a rise in individual real income one would want to say that he or she was better-off. Not only this, but policy makers often have no other measure of well-being. We shall have more to say about the relationship of individual utility and welfare in Chapter 2.

Another line of retreat is to argue that economists and policy makers have typical or average persons in mind, not individuals. The tastes of even average persons change, but not so rapidly as in the case of individuals. They do not rapidly get richer or poorer or

---

[6] I recall Isaiah Berlin saying this about the valid conclusion of some philosophical argument.

suffer from social mobility. They do not marry or get divorced. Most important, they do not die.

However, a rise in average real income is consistent with some people being worse off. We therefore cannot appeal to averages without considering whether it makes sense at all to speak of the general welfare. When some gain but others lose, one cannot logically speak of a general gain or loss without comparing the gains and losses that accrue to different people. Until now we have been considering only the meaning of a rise or fall in utility, and whether it can be reasonably taken to represent a rise or fall in individual well-being. Now that we have adumbrated the more important problem of general well-being we require a new chapter.

2

Collective Utility and Welfare

Through the nineteenth century and beyond, utility was interpreted in terms of happiness or satisfaction. It was implicitly assumed that there was no conceptual problem with maximizing the joint happiness of many persons.[1] The happiness of different persons could be compared, measured in units of utility (utils), and added up (implying cardinal utility). In 1938 Lionel Robbins wrote an article insisting that such interpersonal comparisons were unscientific, and that they were more like judgements of value than judgements of verifiable fact.[2]

Doubtless influenced to some extent by Robbins, economists gave up the idea of cardinal utility, claiming that all the propositions of positive demand theory could be derived from ordinal utility. They even tried to base normative economics on ordinal utility and the incommensurability of individual utilities. Thus one state of affairs was held to be better than another if those who gained *could* overcompensate those who lost. This was unacceptable nonsense, as was soon pointed out. However, the idea of compensation, and its possibilty or otherwise, has remained important in applied welfare economics (that is, cost-benefit analysis—see below). But it was a loss for normative economics that for a decade or more very few economists dared evoke the concept of cardinal utility.

We said in the Introduction that interpersonal comparisons of well-being were best treated as value judgements, although to say that some smiling amiable person is happier than another who goes about with a long face making acid remarks seems much more like a description than a value judgement. But you can never be sure that you are right!

---

[1] Among economists, Jevons was an exception.
[2] E.J. 48 (1938), pp. 640–1.

When Lionel Robbins wrote, logical positivism was in the ascendant, and it was thought that propositions could be easily divided into those with truth values which were descriptive, and those that were properly considered to be expressions of approval or disapproval or some other emotion, and were to be classified as value judgements. But it came to be realized that there were many statements or propositions which were neither clearly one nor the other, but had characteristics of both purely descriptive judgements and value judgements. To say 'X is a cruel man' is a good example. It clearly expresses disapproval and dislike. But equally clearly it differs from 'X is a bad man', for it implies that X has been guilty of some action or actions of a type that could be described as cruel, for instance deliberately causing pain, whereas 'X is a bad man' has no specific reference. So there is a descriptive element in 'X is cruel' although there is no generally accepted criterion of cruelty.

Most interpersonal comparisons are of this mixed type and any controversy over whether they are value judgements or descriptive is futile, for they are often both. What matters is whether there are clear criteria for their truth. Plenty of facts may be adduced which may be persuasive. But where such persuasion is unsuccessful because there are no definite criteria for the truth, then bona fide disagreement is possible. Where such disagreement is passionate, then one can be sure that the contentious statement is relevant to some action or policy, and is a value judgement.

There is no reason in principle why clearly ethical comparisons of differences in states of mind, or states of being, should not be made, and be represented by a cardinal utility function. In practice a person's judgement of goodness or well-being may be less likely to be comprehensive and consistent than his or her choices of baskets of commodities and services, but this is a matter of degree. Propositions are more or less definitely true or false, agreeable or disagreeable.

We saw that in the case of personal utility, a cardinal measure requires the comparison of differences, and not merely levels. Similarly, for a cardinal interpersonal measure of, say, happiness, differences need to be compared. One needs to be able to say for instance, that an extra £1000 a year would make a greater difference to A's happiness than £5000 would to B's happiness. If someone can make many such comparisons consistently, then he is well on the way to using a cardinal measure of the joint happiness of A and B, and similarly for any number of people (of course, this is a big 'if'). To add up the happiness of several persons further requires the definition of zero happiness and a unit of happiness, but this raises no problem of principle. One can, for instance, define zero happiness as that of person A, and the difference of happiness between him or her and B as a unit of happiness.

In recent years happiness has been much studied for its trends, for country comparisons, and for its relation to various situational variables such as real income, education, and democracy.[3] Surveys ask people questions mainly about personal happiness although other nouns may also be used such as subjective well-being (SWB) or general satisfaction. Probably 'happiness' is mostly employed because people are more used to making judgements about happiness than about 'well-being' which is a more professional concept.

In reaching conclusions, which involve averaging over groups, every person's happiness or well-being counts for one. There is thus an implicit interpersonal comparison, obeying Bentham's rule that everyone should count for one. I doubt whether it matters which concept is used. The essential comparative is 'better-off', but 'better-off' has no substantive. Well-being seems the natural choice, and judgements of well-being are clearly both descriptive and value judgements.

There is no doubt that ordinary people such as parents, as well as politicians, bureaucrats, and employers, and everyone who is called upon to make decisions that affect different people differently, often have to make interpersonal comparisons of the kind we are discussing, however limited and sketchy they may be. But the question remains as to how they make them. Even if the well-being of both A and B can be represented by a cardinal utility function we still have to relate A's utility to that of B.

I think most people do this by some form of empathy. People are similar, and one believes that to some extent one can feel as others do, and where there are clearly differences allowances can be made for this. This presumes that utility represents happiness or SWB.[4]

There is a more esoteric approach which puts less emphasis on preferences, and avoids the device of a veil of ignorance. It approaches the subject of welfare more from the direction of moral

[3] See Robert E. Lane, (2000); also Avner Offer (2000). Both contain large bibliographies.   [4] See, for instance, Mirrlees, J.A. (1982).

philosophy than economics. The first stage is to assume that any person's betterness relations can be represented by a cardinal utility index, which requires that these relations obey the axioms of expected utility theory (see Chapter 1). Utility is compared over both states of nature and time. This requires separability in both dimensions, that is the utility of the outcome in one state of nature at a particular time is independent of the outcomes in other states of nature at other times.

But what is the relation of betterness to preferences, or choice? If people always chose what was best for them, a utility index representing choice would, of course, coincide with one representing betterness. What is good for a person surely coincides with his choices to a considerable extent; but, as we have seen, no one would claim that this was always the case. All or almost all prominent utilitarians therefore argue that the coincidence would be perfect only if people were rational, well-informed, and self-interested. It may be objected that people with those characteristics would be different people. So it has to be supposed that everyone's choices are directed by a 'better self' who knows the self-interested tastes of his protegée, but is rational and well-informed.

Generally, commodities are valued by what people will pay for them. But governments often tax and subsidize goods, or regulate their sale, because they wish to discourage or encourage their consumption. Clearly, the government does not consider the social value of a cigarette or a shot of heroin to be their market price. Other items such as works of art may be regarded as having higher social value than people are willing to pay. Within limits, most people will regard some such 'paternalism' as justified: the government takes on the role of one's better self. Applied welfare economics usually recognizes this. Thus a cost-benefit analysis of a project to make cigarettes will value the output net of tax. However, there is nothing objective about what should count as rational for a person, for that depends on the person's goals, and also on an assessment of the probability of the consequences of his or her choices. Who decides then on what influences should be brought to bear on individual choice? In general it is someone in authority, often in reality the government. This basic question of 'who decides' faces us again at the second stage of the approach to the problem of how to pass from the welfare of individuals to general welfare.

Individual utility is thus somehow defined to be an increasing function of good, and higher utility implies better. But, although itself cardinal the utility function need not represent good cardinally. This leaves room for the individual to be risk averse (or risk loving) about goodness. Although by definition economic man maximizes expected utility, he or she may not maximize expected goodness.

The second stage is to posit a general betterness relation ordering all possible outcomes for all persons at all times. This relation is also assumed to conform to the axioms of expected utility theory, and to obey the Pareto-like rule that one general outcome is better than another if, and only if, at least one person is better-off and none worse off.

Some mathematical wizardry then proves the remarkable result that general betterness can be represented by an expectational utility function that is the sum of expectational utility functions representing the betterness relations of individuals. The shape of the individual utility functions representing betterness is determined by attitudes to risk. These same functions, defined to represent good for people in the face of uncertainty about states of nature, also determine what is good when aggregating across people. General utility may thus be a concave function of personal goods, meaning that more good for a person with a lot of good counts for less than an equal addition for someone with less good.

In Chapter 1 we suggested a relation between risk aversion and a preference for equality by using the device of choosing a social system from behind a veil of ignorance. We now have the same result arising from the logic of aggregating goodness over both states of nature and persons.

The above sketchy account of how the goods of different individuals may be aggregated—the 'interpersonal addition theorem'—is taken from John Broome[5] and is an amended version of a theory due to John Harsanyi.[6] The assumptions needed are formidable. Comparability of personal welfare is, of course, assumed.

---

[5] John Broome, *Weighing Goods*, 1991. This brilliant book is devoted to the rigorous derivation of the 'interpersonal addition theorem' as he terms it. It contains full references to other contributors.

[6] Harsanyi, John C. (1955). See also Peter J. Hammond (1982).

We have already seen that there is a problem in influencing actual choices to make it more plausible that A is better than B if A is chosen rather than B. The same problem of 'who decides?' emerges with interpersonal comparisons of good. We do not suppose that there is some objective general betterness relation (or 'social welfare function'). There is certainly room for bona fide disagreement about many interpersonal comparisons. So who decides whether an outcome which is good for one person and bad for another is good in general? The answer in principle is 'you do'! In practice for applied welfare economics the answer is 'some authority' or 'the government'. There are other more technical assumptions. All choices from uncertain prospects are made assuming the same probabilities. Separability across persons and states of nature is also needed, that is the goodness of an outcome for a particular person in a particular state of nature must be unaffected by the outcomes for all other persons in this and other states.

A famous result, using interpersonal cardinal utility, is that of Mirrlees.[7] Tom and Dick have the same utility functions with diminishing marginal utility of income and leisure, which is not an inferior good. But Tom is more productive than Dick. Maximum utility requires Tom to work longer hours than Dick, and receive less income to the point where he is less well-off. Such a radical redistribution is surprising, and could come about only under a discerning overseer with a whip, for otherwise Tom would hide his ability. This result may make one doubt whether one would wish utility to be maximized in all circumstances.

It may seem that the interpersonal addition theorem has achieved all that utilitarians demand—that the general welfare can be regarded as a sum of individual well-beings. This is not so if utilitarianism is taken to mean that utility, representing happiness or well-being, is to be maximized regardless of the interpersonal distribution of levels of well-being. We have seen that if individual expectational utilities, representing goodness, are risk averse, then equality has some value. For utilitarianism to follow, this must be ruled out. This implies accepting what John Broome calls Bernouilli's hypothesis to the effect that 'one alternative is at least as good for a person as another if and only if it gives the person at

---

[7] Mirrlees *loc cit*. The result is proved in Mirrlees 'Notes on Welfare Economics, Information and Uncertainty' in M.S. Balch, D. McFadden, and S.Y. Wu (eds), 1974.

least as great an expectation of her good'.[8] Given this neutrality concerning 'goodness risk', the utility function represents the person's good cardinally, and its maximization maximizes good. The general good can then be represented as the addition of individual goods, which is the central tenet of utilitarianism.

John Broome finds separability in time especially difficult to swallow. A person's life may be divided into a number of periods, with amounts of good assigned to each period. These amounts are independent of each other. But a person does not consist simply of the sum of himself of herself in each period. For instance, from the point of view of the person's whole life, a smaller total of good might be preferred to a larger total of periodic ups and downs. Others may find more difficulty with interpersonal than with intertemporal additions, and indeed may refuse to admit interpersonal comparability of goodness at all. Or, again, some may refuse to agree that utility can be measured, or if it can be measured that it can represent goodness. In short, the theory cannot be regarded as compelling. Nevertheless, although not compelling it is permissive. An observer cannot be condemned for uttering necessarily nonsensical statements if he speaks of aggregate well-being.

We have been discussing collective well-being on the implicit assumption that the collective is an unchanging group of persons. We have thus ignored matters of life and death. Unsurprisingly these are of importance for both individuals and governments. Most people make decisions about trying to have children and trying not to have them. They also decide on health expenditure and numerous other matters that affect their expectations of life. Doctors may have to decide whose life to try hardest to save, and whether to practise euthanasia. Governments are also deeply involved. Most public expenditures will affect the expectations of life of many citizens. They will be called upon to have a population policy, and to pass laws about birth control. The government of a state is also required to define its membership, and to have some immigration policies.

In all these problems arising from changes in the community, especially those of life and death, moral philosophy and economics are closely entwined. Politics is also usually involved. For this

---

[8] John Broome *ibid*. p. 142.

reason they can be best discussed only after a critique of utilitarianism (in the past they have been mostly discussed in a utilitarian
framework) and of 'rights' theories, topics which we discuss
in Part II. Meanwhile we turn to the subject of welfare economics
in Chapter 3.

3

Welfare Economics

The first point to make is that welfare economics is not the economics of the Welfare State, as any non-economist forgivably tends to think. It is any part of economics that relates to the well-being or welfare of a group of persons, where the group may comprise any number from two to all the citizens of some nation-state, or even everyone or every sentient being in the world. In short, it is all parts of economics that implicitly or explicitly use the concept of collective well-being that was discussed in Chapter 2. Welfare economics is obviously very closely related to normative economics which is concerned with what ought to be done: and more generally with economic policy. It can be divided into theoretical and applied branches.

THEORETICAL WELFARE ECONOMICS

Theoretical welfare economics derives necessary conditions for the achievement of a 'Pareto-optimum'. A Pareto-optimum is defined as a situation where it is impossible to make one person better-off without making some other person worse-off. More or less utility, as discussed in Chapter 1, is the criterion of better-offness.

The simplest case is that of exchange between two individuals with either different possessions or different tastes. First, they are not allowed to trade. Then barriers are lifted and some trade takes place. They are then both better-off, other things being equal, because they have reached positions chosen rather than what they had before. They traded because their relative marginal valuations of the traded commodities differed. They traded until these valuations were equalized, or until one of them ran out of the good he was selling. The necessary condition for a Pareto-optimum is that their relative marginal valuations of any pair of goods that both use should be equal. Economists have derived many similar conditions for production and consumption: they all involve the equalization of marginal valuations. In general, a Pareto-optimum requires the simultaneous satisfaction of all such conditions.

The jewel in the crown of theoretical welfare economics is that a competitive equilibrium is Pareto-optimal. It is important to assess the real moral and practical importance of this glittering result, which was dimly sensed by Adam Smith but rigorously proved only after 1950.[1]

We shall not in this chapter pursue any difficulties arising from the changing nature of the community under consideration. We here assume a constant set of persons over a given period of time: what is inherited from earlier periods and bequeathed to later periods is predetermined. The essential feature of perfect competition is that the buyer or seller cannot affect the price of what is bought and sold. This is no place for an assessment of how far this either is or could be true of a modern economy: but it must be obvious to any casual observer that it is not exactly true over wide areas of the economy, especially in manufacturing and the supply of utilities. Whether it is true enough for practical policy purposes is often contentious. Whether it could be true partly depends on technology. Increasing returns (costs fall as production increases) may preclude competition. Where this is the case, regulation is often instituted to prevent the supplier being able to set the price.

There are other problems. Since exchanges are rarely simultaneous they will take place only if each participant trusts the other to fulfil his part of the bargain. The problem of mistrust is further discussed in Chapter 9. More generally, many contracts involve the future; and future prices exist only for a few commodities so that the prices that are supposed to guide the economy to an optimum outcome do not always exist. Another demanding requirement is the absence of 'externalities'. This term of art applies whenever someone who is not a party to a particular transaction or activity gains or loses thereby. If a supplier of some service cannot charge everyone who enjoys it, that is, to use current jargon, if there are *free-riders* there is an externality. If a firm uses scarce resources without adequate payment, for example, using a river as a drain; or creates costs for others by spewing out dirty smoke, we have examples of external diseconomies. Textbook examples usually concern

---

[1] See Arrow, K. and G. Debreu 'Existence of an Equilibrium for a Competitive Economy', *Econometrica*, 22, 1954.

production and exchange: and these are relevant to the welfare theorem that pure competition leads to a Pareto-optimum. The best way of dealing with such externalities, to make the theorem more likely to approximate the truth, is part of the subject of applied welfare economics. But there are also externalities that may have nothing to do with production or exchange. Excessive noise is the salient example, since very loud sound reproduction has become technically possible and popular.

Public goods are the most important example of a case where private production may be imposible because of free-riders, as those who use a service without paying are called. One cannot recover the cost of a lighthouse from selling its services. Anyone can get a fix on the light for free: no one can be *excluded*. More importantly, national defence cannot be divided into small parcels and sold to individuals, and, once provided, no one can be excluded from its protection.

The existence of public goods precludes the possibility of obtaining a Pareto-optimum via competition, because they cannot themselves be competitively produced. But their interference is more radical than that. They have to be paid for by taxation, and all taxation in practice prevents the equality of the marginal valuations that is required for the attainment of a Pareto-optimum. For instance, if there is a tax, such as income tax, that falls on earnings, those affected will tend to work less and have more leisure than they would choose if there were no tax; or, often more realistically, they will find paid employment which the revenue does not detect. Economists have invented a kind of tax they call *lump sum* which is unrelated to any economic choice people may make, and therefore cannot distort choice, a distortion that prevents the attainment of a Pareto-optimum. Unfortunately, in general, such taxes do not exist.

The subject of public goods is such a large part of any discussion of the proper role of government that we defer further discussion to Chapter 9. But before leaving the subject of theoretical welfare economics, the importance (or unimportance) of the concept of a Pareto-optimum needs further comment. Suppose one starts with a Pareto-optimum. There is no way of making Paul better off without harming someone. Now suppose we harm Peter by removing resources from him in an amount that he cannot influence in any way—that is, by a lump sum tax (see above). We give these resources to Paul (a lump sum subsidy). Peter and Paul, and everyone else, can now produce and trade freely. Given the assumptions we have discussed, they reach a new Pareto-optimum. It is obvious that there is an infinite number of such Pareto-optima. They cannot be ordered in terms of goodness without some comparison of states of affairs in which some are better-off and others worse-off. The same is true of sub-optimal states of affairs. In particular, any Pareto-optimum can be worse than many states of affairs that are sub-optimal. These states can all be ordered in terms of their goodness only if there is a 'general betterness relation' as discussed in Chapter 2.[2]

APPLIED WELFARE ECONOMICS AND COST-BENEFIT ANALYSIS

In moving from theoretical to applied welfare economics we move essentially from necessary conditions for optimum states of affairs, and how such optima may be achieved, to problems that involve deciding whether one actual state of affairs is better or worse than another.

Cost-benefit analysis compares states of affairs with and without the project that is being analysed. It is applied welfare economics. Indeed it comprises almost all that is of interest in applying welfare economics. This may surprise some sociologists who identify cost-benefit analysis with the number crunching and undue influence of economists who have no understanding or concern for human welfare. This identification is a mistake.

Cost-benefit analysis began with the evaluation of water-resource investments in the USA in the 1930s, and was fathered by engineers rather than economists. It has spread widely but is still mainly thought of as a technique for the evaluation of public sector investment projects. What the economists try to calculate is whether or not the gainers from the project could at least compensate those who would lose. They may also be called upon to identify the winners and the losers. Whenever the consequences of a project for the well-being of those affected directly or indirectly by it are of importance for the decision, whether or not to approve the project, then cost-benefit analysis is the only logical method.

---

[2] 'General betterness relation' is a concept employed by John Broome (1991). In most works on theoretical welfare economics the same purpose is effected by what is termed a 'social welfare function' (SWF).

Although formal cost-benefit calculations seem to be largely confined to investment projects, the method may be applied, however roughly and informally, to any decision by any agent, public or private. This is why we have said that cost-benefit analysis comprises almost all that is of interest in applying welfare economics.

Let us return to the problem posed by the fact that what the economist or the team of project appraisers tries to calculate is only whether the gainers could compensate the losers, or, what usually comes to almost the same thing, whether the project has a positive present social value (PSV).[3] We have in effect already strongly argued that a positive PSV does not entail an improvement. If there are any losers, a distributional judgement is still required to the effect that the benefits outweigh the losses *in terms of welfare*.[4]

Some economists try to evade the logical necessity of a distributional value judgement. Some feel that economics becomes unscientific if value judgements are admitted: they are trying to fly without wings. Others, more reasonably, argue that these interpersonal judgements require a lot of research as to who gains and loses and by how much, and that mostly those who lose on the swings will anyway gain on the roundabouts. Moreover, where public projects are in question, distributional considerations may come to the fore to an undesirable extent, especially as the political authority that delivers judgement is likely to be more interested in votes than in

[3] Present value (PV) is the total estimated discounted monetary value of all receipts less expenditures. Cost-benefit analysis is normally aimed at establishing the present *social* value of a project (PSV), and it is this that is required to show that the gainers could compensate the losers. We have said in the text that positive PSV is almost the same as saying that the gainers could compensate the losers. We say 'almost' if only because the losers may be uncompensatable, for instance if they are dead.

PV and PSV differ in so far as, (1) actual prices do not reflect social values, and (2) there are externalities. The analyst may allow for the first problem by using accounting prices which are calculated to be equal to social values, and for the second by attributing a value to the supposed externalities. The problems involved are examined at book length in I.M.D. Little and J.A. Mirrlees, *Project Appraisal and Planning for Developing Countries.*

[4] A dual criterion for an economic improvement that included a distributional judgement was proposed in I.M.D. Little, *A Critique of Welfare Economics* (second edition, 1957). Much misunderstanding ensued. In 'Welfare Criteria, Distribution, and Cost Benefit Analysis' in Michael J. Boskin (ed.), *Economics and Human Welfare*, Little claims that this 'Little Criterion' is valid and useful, and is in fact the basis of most cost-benefit analysis.

welfare. There is much to be said for this point of view. Progress would surely be inhibited, to the cost of nearly everyone, if all run-of-the-mill investment projects, or changes of policy or practice, whether in the public or private sectors, had to be the subject of a distributional analysis and judgement.

But there is a difference between saying that all projects require a distributional judgement, and that none do. Both statements are, in my opinion, wrong. Large public sector infrastructural projects, whatever the general benefit, often harm many. Dams, flooding whole valleys and depriving hundreds or thousands of people of their homes and livelihoods, are a *cause celebre*. In such cases, of course, compensation should be paid but it may be very difficult or impossible for it to be adequate.

In some cases, the distributional judgement is the heart of the matter. Any general benefit or harm may be very small or irrelevant. Whether to save the life of A or B, is an example if the decision is made solely on grounds of which person's utility loss is greater (compensation is not possible!). But if A is an inventive scientist, and there is nothing much to be said in favour of B, then a social cost-benefit analysis might swing the decision in favour of A. A dual criterion would again be needed.

PART II

POLITICS AND
PHILOSOPHY

4

The Role of the State

In Part I we saw that a distributional judgement may be needed in order to determine whether one state of affairs is better than another. It is sufficient for such a judgement to be needed that somebody is worse off in the situation that is putatively better.

We now address the question 'who makes the judgement?'. One answer we have already suggested is 'you make it'. Anyone is free to make such a moral judgement. Another answer given by several political philosophers is that an impartial observer makes it: impartiality is supposedly assured by placing the hypothetical observer behind a 'veil of ignorance' so that he does not know what position he would occupy in the various states of affairs (see page 6). These are armchair answers.

However, in this chapter we are interested in real life decisions, and have to ask who makes them. It may be someone in his personal capacity. An obvious example is that of a person deciding, say, whether to leave his estate to his son or to charity. At the other extreme it is the state or some organ of the state that has the authority to decide. In between, there are many private organizations empowered to make decisions that have distributional consequences. Although these latter may involve politics (local politics, university politics, ecclesiastical politics, etc.), we shall in this chapter concentrate on the state. This is because we shall be particularly interested in the limits, if any, to a state's authority and in its legitimate aims: whereas the powers of nongovernmental organizations, operating within the jurisdiction of a state, are limited by the law, while their aims are usually fairly closely defined.

Before proceeding we must say something about the concept of a state, and of government. The state comprises all the legislative, executive, and judicial institutions; and the laws (including the constitution, if any), governing the inhabitants of the territory to which it lays claim. It is also often defined by the claims that its agents make. It thereby claims to be the sole final maker of laws, and to be the final judge and sole executive. In particular it claims a monopoly of the use of force both over its own citizens, and over foreigners (only it can declare war).

Governments may be thought of as tenants of the state. They come and go, either violently or in accordance with the constitution or customs of the state. While in office a government may change the institutions and laws of the state (including the constitution) in accordance with the constitution: but at any given moment it is the agent of the state. For this reason, although it is usually the executive branch of the government, or some agent of it, that makes the decisions that interest us, we shall mostly concern ourselves with the state as if there was no distinction to be drawn between government and state.

LIMITATIONS OF STATE AUTHORITY

We next ask what, if any, are the boundaries to the state's authority; and what legal and moral constraints there are on its decision-making. Are there some kinds of private activity it should never interfere with? Are there state actions that are morally repugnant, and what are their characteristics? What would justify disobedience and rebellion?

To some extent, states may limit themselves by a constitution. The USA is the prime example. Not only is the USA a federation, which limits the power of the federal government, but also federal executive power is limited by the bicameral legislature, whose powers are in turn limited by the constitution as interpreted by the Supreme Court. The founding fathers were very much concerned with the declared rights of the citizen when they originated such a complex system of 'checks and balances', limiting centralized sovereignty.

But what can it mean to say that a person or institution controls or limits itself? A constitution has been likened to a chastity belt whose wearer knows the whereabouts of the key. Alternatively, the sovereign power of the state would seem to be limited only by the fact that its incumbent government may be overthrown by violent if not by constitutional means. Even then the state may continue virtually unchanged. Be that as it may, no amount of actual self-restraint by the state makes redundant the question of what limits there ought to be to its powers; and what limits there are to the obligation of citizens, or residents of the state's territory, to obey the state. These are the traditional questions of political philosophy.

The very idea that a state's powers should be limited implies that its subjects have rights which the state ought not to subvert or trample on; that there are things that the state must not do to anyone. But the meaning of rights, if such there be, and their origin or derivation is controversial. Some extended discussion is essential.

INDIVIDUAL RIGHTS

If rights are to protect people from excessive interference by the state it is clear that they cannot derive from the state. Where then do they come from? Some may believe that they come from God. But throughout this book we take an atheistic point of view. Perhaps they come from nowhere! Such rights as are not clearly created by the state or by individuals themselves (see below) are variously referred to as 'natural', 'basic', or 'human' rights. They somehow inhere in human beings. This view has been ridiculed. Bentham famously referred to natural rights as 'nonsense on stilts'. More recently Ronald Dworkin refers to a US judge who thought it a sufficient refutation of a judicial philosophy he disliked to point out that it rested on the preposterous notion that natural rights were 'spectral attributes worn by primitive men, like amulets, which they carry into civilization to ward off tyranny'.[1]

Hart has defended a concept of minimal natural rights, that is the right to be free. More accurately, he claims that if there are any moral rights at all, 'any adult human being capable of choice, (1) has the right to forbearance on the part of all others from the use of coercion or restraint against him save to hinder coercion or restraint, and (2) is at liberty to do (i.e. is under no obligation to abstain from) any action which is not one of coercing or restraining or designed to injure other persons'.[2]

There are several points to note. First, there is the reservation 'if there are any moral rights'. Hart made this reservation because it is possible to imagine a moral code which contains no reference to

---

[1] R. Dworkin *Taking Rights Seriously*, Duckworth, 1978, p. 176.
[2] H.L.A. Hart 'Are there any natural rights', *Philosophical Review*, 64 (1955), pp. 175–91, reprinted in Anthony Quinton (ed.), *Political Philosophy*, OUP, 1967.

rights. Second, the second clause although part of what Hart meant by a natural right, is stated as a liberty not as a right. If natural rights are thus identified with liberties it follows that a person has a vast range of natural rights—to breathe, blink, stand up, sit down, and so on. I think that those who want to insist on natural, human, and basic rights, would want to restrict such rights to actions of some moral importance. Also, the word 'likely' should be substituted for 'designed' in this clause. Speed limits are justified when fast driving is likely to injure others: design or intent is not necessary. Third, the first clause gives anyone who wants to claim natural rights as a defence against excessive interference by the state all that he or she could want, provided that 'all others' includes the state. Hart goes on to say that the above right, which he also describes as the right to be free, belongs to all men *qua* men, and not only if they are members of some society, or stand in some special relation to each other. I find this puzzling. It is hard to think of a human being who is not a member of some society. Equally, it is hard to think of a moral code existing without society (or society existing without a moral code). Indeed it seems to me to be nonsense. Thus rights and forbearance from coercion imply a moral code, and a moral code implies society.

But belonging to a society is not the same as being a citizen of a state. Society, which may be no more than a family or a clan, existed before states, that is before the emergence of authoritative institutions claiming a monopoly of force and effectively demanding obedience. Conventions and moral codes evolved and became an essential component of all societies; they ruled, or at least strongly influenced, man's behaviour to man. Hobbes was wrong to think that life without Leviathan was necessarily 'solitary, poore, nasty, brutish and short'.[3] Rights thus exist independently of any state.

Hart classified rights as specific or general. Specific rights exist only when there is a special relation between people. The paradigm is a promise or a contract (which is a mutual promise). When one promises someone something, the promisee acquires a right that the promiser does what he promises. The promiser creates this right, and also an obligation to do what he or she promises. They may also arise from conventions. In a particular situation, when two people are about to collide, there may be a convention determining

[3] Thomas Hobbes, *Leviathan*, London, 1651, p. 97.

which has the right of way. The other is then obliged to give way. In such circumstances the convention may be interpreted as an implicit agreement in so far as it benefits everyone subject to the convention.[4] All specific rights are matched by obligations; and obligations exist only as a counterpart to someone having a right. One might add that specific legal rights with corresponding obligations may be conferred by the state. This is not, I think, controversial.

However, the idea of general rights is difficult. They are supposed to be examples of what Hart has called the right to be free—such rights as the right to speak one's mind, to worship as one pleases, to walk about, and to breathe. The trouble with using 'rights' in this way is that a person is free to do anything which is not prohibited by the accepted customs and conventions, or laws, of society; and so there is an infinite list of rights. It is redundant to refer to the right to be free: one is simply free.

Isaiah Berlin has referred to human rights as constituting 'a frontier of freedom' which no person or government should be allowed to cross. He argues that the rules defining this frontier '... are accepted so widely, and are grounded so deeply in the cultural nature of men as they have developed through history, as to be, by now, an essential part of what we mean by being a normal human being'.[5] This is acceptable, except that an infinite list of rights is not convincing as a frontier. The frontier is properly constituted by the quite limited list of things that one may not do to human beings.

The first resounding sentence of Robert Nozick's *Anarchy, State and Utopia* is 'individuals have rights, and there are things no person or group may do to them (without violating their rights)'. Some emphasis but no sense would have been lost if he had written 'There are things no person or group may do to individuals'. Critics have rightly complained that Nozick does not explain the source of the rights to which he refers. But the prohibitions are not derived from rights. If instead we ask what is the source of these prohibitions—the things one may not do to people—the answer is easy. The source is the set of customs and conventions that have grown in all societies, probably from even before beings became human. The prohibitions are, in the main, those against killing,

---

[4] See R. Sugden (1998).   [5] *Four Essays on Liberty*, p. 165.

maiming, and attacking people, and stealing their property. These are customs and conventions that are essential for any viable society.

General rights can thus be eliminated by wielding Ockham's razor—'entities are not to be multiplied beyond necessity'. It is logically more economical to use the concept of wrongdoing: it is wrong to interfere with a person's freedom except to prevent him wronging others. However, on occasion, it may be useful to stress a prohibition by appealing to a right, for example free speech. We shall also find it convenient sometimes to use the phrase 'property rights' (see below).[6]

We have so far considered only the rights, obligations, and duties of individuals. What rights and duties does the state have?[7] This question brings us in the next section to a consideration of the idea of a social contract. But, first, let us make it clear that we assume that state rights and duties, if any, derive from individuals. This is to deny the doctrine of communitarianism. Communitarians believe that there is a common good which resides, as it were, in a community and is not reducible to individual goods. Indeed, individuals do not exist apart from the community and natural rights are nonsense.

The 'good of the community' is a seductive phrase for some. For others it threatens to give the state (or any governing body) the right to do anything regardless of all harm to individuals; and this smacks of totalitarianism and tyranny. This may be unfair, and we consider communitarianism more fully in Chapter 8. But we revert in this chapter to the point of view that we have maintained throughout, called 'methodological individualism'. It claims that the costs and benefits of all public goods can be reduced to those of individuals.

SOCIAL CONTRACT AND PROPERTY

That state rights and duties derive from individuals is implied by the theory of the social contract, which goes back in modern times

---

[6] In insisting on wrongs as morally more fundamental than rights I have been much influenced by Jasay. See also the section on justice in Chapter 5.

[7] Institution, apart from the state, may make contracts and so acquire duties and rights. The legal conditions under which they may do so need not concern us. The question of whether groups which are not institutions with constitutions and responsible agents, can have rights is arguable.

at least to Hobbes. Hobbes envisaged people forming a covenant to institute a sovereign power that would ensure the security lacking in a state of nature. Once instituted this sovereign reigned supreme. Its subjects had no rights to overthrow it, for the state was the source of all morality. We shall, however, take John Locke as our guide since his account of the social contract is fuller and permits discussion of human rights and political obligation (with Hobbes obedience was paramount).[8]

Locke's state of nature was more pleasant than that of Hobbes. A moral code with rights and duties existed. These rights came from God. Nevertheless people could not be trusted, and hence security was a serious problem. Therefore they traded away their natural rights under a contract whereby the state acquired a duty to protect those same rights. The specified rights were those of life, liberty, and property. If the state failed in its duty, its subjects would be morally justified in rebelling. Correspondingly, the citizens acquired a duty to obey unless the state failed in its duty to protect their lives, liberty, and property.

There are grave problems with any contract theory (contractarianism), and this includes recent theories such as that of John Rawls and other contractarians, which we examine in Chapters 6 and 7. The contract is, of course, hypothetical; no one supposes that states began with an actual contract. But how can a hypothetical contract impose obligations on actual people, or give the state any rights? Resort may be had to an implicit contract, such as that which, economists say, describes the informal relationship between employer and employee. But such contracts arise between free agents, while most people do not choose to be members of the state. With some states they have not even been free to leave. The idea of an implicit contract seems to apply better to a tourist than a citizen. It may be argued that the benefits of protection by the state impose some duties on the citizen, but that argument need not depend on any contract. Finally, some people may fear that contractarianism tends to limit, without good reason, the function of the state to the maintenance of law and order and the protection of property.

If we dismiss the idea of a social contract we have to ask whence comes the state's right or freedom to do anything. Our position is that all rights are created or conferred by social interaction.

[8] J. Locke *Two Treatises of Government*, P. Laslett (ed.), OUP, 1960.

An individual is free to confer rights on others, and create obligations for himself. This may be done by explicit promise or contract; but it is also possible to behave in such a way as to create legitimate expectations, which amount to a right to expect. That an individual can create rights springs from social convention and custom. One must not ask 'What right has a person to create rights?' That way lies a regress into madness.

Institutions such as firms, schools, clubs, and local governments, can also create rights and obligations. However, partly because these institutions are social creations and not moral persons, their powers are usually closely defined by law.

The state is an institution. It differs from other institutions in that it claims a monopoly of coercion by force which is a liberty denied to other institutions or persons except by delegation from itself. However, this does not imply that a state's exclusive freedom to use force to prevent or punish wrongdoing is an exception to our contention that rights are created by social interaction. In whatever way states were created, they have become part of, a rather important part of, the social framework. No more than is the case with individuals should we ask 'By what right does the state create rights and accept obligations?' But we can, and should, question whether particular state rights, and obligations or duties, have been clearly established; and whether they are morally acceptable. This in no way differs from conventional rights and duties that do not involve the state.

It is useful to consider further the rights of life, liberty, and property which Locke considered as the function of the state to protect. Rights to life and liberty are exactly those rights that Hart considered to be natural general rights. We have cast doubt on this usage of 'rights'. But it comes to the same thing to maintain that a function of the state is to prevent wrongdoing. It is implicit that the state should not itself do wrong. *Prima facie* it thus has no right to coerce people except to prevent them doing wrong, or punishing them for it.

Certainly, states claim exceptions. The state demands people's lives in time of war, and most people probably think it has a right to do so. Liberty is always arguable. An individual's liberty, whether in a pre-state society or under a state, is conditional on not trespassing on the liberty of others, including harming or killing them. But the extent of the coercion that is appropriate to stop coercion, which surely depends on the amount of harm done or likely to occur, is hard to decide. Who decides? Ultimately it is the state, as always. I think no one contests this, although there is often violent disagreement in particular cases (as I write, the treatment of pae-dophiles is the occasion of ugly violence). Finally, the state claims the right to tax some people, or restrict their freedom, in order to benefit others. It is a claim that the state has a right to do things which no individual has a right to do. (We discuss it further below.)

PROPERTY AND PROPERTY RIGHTS

We have argued that a person is free to do anything that is not wrong, where wrongdoing is defined by the customs, conventions, and laws of society. If some behaviour is wrong in this sense we shall, for brevity, call it socially unacceptable; and if not wrong, socially acceptable. A person's freedom must clearly include use of his property, which includes parts of his body such as his fist, and personal possessions such as his boot or his gun. There is essent-ially no difference between personal freedom and freedom to use personal property. We shall for convenience sometimes use the phrase 'property rights' as shorthand for freedom to use property in any way that is socially acceptable.

Some uses of property, especially land, are quite severely res-tricted. A landowner is seldom allowed to erect buildings without permission. He may not be allowed to cut trees, grow certain crops, keep certain animals, and so on. These restrictions may be made because some uses of land are thought to create external disec-onomies. Sometimes they are made in pursuit of some central economic plan. The occupier of land may also not be free to sell it to anyone, or bequeath it. The question then arises whether he or she really owns it, or is perhaps a tenant of the state.

It is the concept of *ownership* of property, not property rights, that is troublesome. How does it come about that someone acquires freedom to use some object or idea as he will, subject only to such use being socially acceptable, or legal.[9] The most common way of acquiring property is by working: no one contests that a person owns the proceeds of selling his or her services. A person may also make money by using other assets: if these were acquired without

---

[9] Property in ideas, and intellectual property in general, has special features which we decline to discuss for lack of space and expertise.

any wrongdoing, no further problem arises. Acquisition by exchange also presents no problem if the exchange was freely entered into and the object or asset received was indeed the property of the other party. An exception is that, nowadays, one may not acquire a slave; and a person is not free to sell himself into slavery.

Much the same is true of gifts, including inheritance. Inheritance comes under attack because the heir did not himself earn the value of the property acquired. His father or grandfather or someone many generations ago may have earned it and was free to bequeath it. But then again, it is possible that no one did. Land, including all natural assets, is the source of the problem because no one made it, and so no one could have acquired it by making it. How was land appropriated in the first instance? At one time it can be supposed that land was free, and that individual ownership was unknown. At some point, land was enclosed, individual ownership claimed, and exclusion of others successfully enforced. This development doubtless came about for economic reasons: as land became scarce it was more efficiently used when individual ownership ruled.[10] Does the encloser acquire a property right?

Locke had an answer. The answer was 'yes', provided that 'enough and as good was left for others'. Most economists would agree that no property rights could be claimed in this way, for if land was not scarce at the time it might become so, and if there was no expectation of scarcity it would not have been enclosed. One could never be sure that 'Locke's Proviso' as it is called, was satisfied. It seems likely that most land was in fact appropriated by conquest, seizure, and enclosure. Even when enclosure resulted in large productivity gains, it is very unlikely that no one lost.

While any property, not merely natural resources, may be tainted by unjustified acquisition somewhere on the line of its historial descent, it would be extreme to argue that all property is theft, as Proudhon maintained.[11] At some point the evils of the past have to be forgotten and ownership recognized.

Nozick, whose entitlement theory of justice relies heavily on just acquisition, admits that much past acquisition harmed many people.[12] He proposes a principle of 'rectification'. Obviously the individual descendants of those ravaged by Ghengis Khan or British colonizers cannot be identified and compensated. Nor can

[10] See Demsetz (1967).   [11] P.-J. Proudhon (1840).   [12] R. Nozick (1974).

the descendants of the original invaders be made to pay. Recognizing this, Nozick suggests that poor people are most probably the descendants of those who originally suffered.[13] This seems to be a highly dubious attempt to reconcile welfare payments with the author's denial of the state's right to redistribute on utilitarian grounds.

Restitution is, however, a live issue. North American Indians, Aborigines in Australia, and other indigenous peoples, claim restitution, or at least compensation, for loss of land and minerals many generations ago. There are, however, philosophical difficulties. The claims are on behalf of tribes or larger ethnic groups, not individuals. This presumes the questionable claim that groups can have moral rights and duties and that they can be bequeathed to later generations. Moreover, the claimant tribe would also need to show that it itself acquired the land without harming others. This is not to say that more should not be done for some such groups, but only that the case that it would be a restitution of rights is dubious.[14]

We have already seen that private property in land came about, at least in some cases, for reasons of productive efficiency, that is more would be produced from the same resources. It is now generally recognized that a clear definition of property is essential for economic efficiency. The harm that results from common usage of scarce resources—for example, over-fishing—is well known. Clear definitions of property may also eliminate some reputed failures of the price mechanism.[15] Of course, all property, except perhaps toothbrushes, might be public and ownership clearly defined. A socialist factory manager may know precisely what is his and what is not, and what he is allowed to do with what is his. But economic inefficiency would then have different grounds, which we need not elaborate.

Our discussion of property rights is a prelude to whether they constitute a defence against actions of the state which appear to infringe them. First, however, let us summarize the discussion thus far. Property exists. That something is mine and not yours is a moral claim and not merely a legal claim. You have no right to take it from me. It is mine if I acquired it by working; or by exchange or gift provided the other party in turn owned it. It is an open question how far such ownership need be traced. I would suggest not

---

[13] *Ibid.* p. 231. [14] See David Lyons (1982). [15] See Coase (1960).

further than one transaction. My sins may impose a duty of restitution on my children, but not my grandchildren: and certainly not indefinitely. Ownership implies that the owner is free to use the property in any way that is socially acceptable. The state has a right to pass and enforce laws to prevent socially unacceptable uses. But the state also has a duty to protect the owner's property and his freedom to use it in socially acceptable ways. The state is certainly not protecting property by removing it, without due judicial cause such as a fine imposed for unacceptable behaviour. It appears therefore that the state has no right to impose taxes, or other restraints, for the purpose of redistribution. This is a conclusion that most people would not accept.

What can those who favour redistributory policies say? If not living in a wholly socialized economy, where redistribution would not be an issue, they can hardly deny individual ownership, or deny that taxation for the sole purpose of taking property away from some to give to others is an infringement of the former's freedom. There is no way out for the apologist of such redistribution except to say that the state's duty to protect property does not always apply to its own takings. If every infringement of rights entails an injustice, it follows that the state ought to be unjust for the purpose of some redistribution. This is an uncomfortable statement, but it is not a contradiction. It is what I believe myself. The alternative is to state that actions which would be unjust if carried out for any other reason may not be unjust if the purpose is to improve welfare by redistribution. There is no significant difference. Put either way, the upshot is that welfare may sometimes trump justice.

We have now introduced the notion of redistribution as a possible aim of the state which goes beyond its duty to preserve law and order, and protect property. In Chapters 5 and 6 we turn to an examination of theories which, it is claimed, justify a more interventionist state. The first of these is utilitarianism.

5

Utilitarianism: Theory and Applications

In modern times the doctrine goes back at least as far as Francis Hutcheson,[1] and David Hume,[2] who saw justice and morality as rooted in utility, meaning by utility whatever is valuable for society. But Jeremy Bentham is generally taken to be the founder of utilitarianism as a comprehensive principle by which the greatest amount of happiness was an end that should guide the actions of both individuals and governments.

If utility is taken to mean happiness, utilitarianism goes back to Aristotle. To quote '... let us say what we claim to be the aim of political science—that is, of all the good things to be done what is the highest. Most people, I should think, agree about what it is called, since both the masses and sophisticated people call it happiness, understanding being happy as equivalent to living well and acting well'.[3]

We have in Chapter 2 explained how utility can be thought of as representing collective happiness or well-being. We shall not go further into the difficulties discussed in Chapter 2, but explore objections to the principle of maximizing happiness or welfare, assuming that it makes sense to think of amounts of happiness at different times. Following tradition we sometimes use the concept of happiness, but utility can be defined so as to represent the good of both individuals and society directly. So we may also refer to maximizing welfare or the good.

Utilitarianism is a version of consequentialism which asserts that whether an action is right or wrong depends *solely* on the goodness of its consequences, and it has been attacked for this

---

[1] *A System of Moral Philosophy*, 1755.
[2] *An Enquiry Concerning the Principles of Morals*, 1751, reprinted (1983), J.B. Schneewind (ed.).   [3] *Nicomachean Ethics*, CUP 2000, p. 5.

reason. Consequentialism has been held to ignore much that is of moral importance such as rights, duties, and obligations, virtue, integrity, and deserts. Utilitarianism has some good answers.

First we must discuss the distinction that has been drawn between Act and Rule Utilitarianism. Rule Utilitarianism was invented as an answer to the objection that utilitarianism, a variety of consequentialism, ignored important moral rules.[4] It was held that some rules are essential for the general welfare. An act whose consequences might seem to maximize utility, but which broke such a rule, could undermine the general adherence to rules which are essential for a peaceful and thriving society. An obvious example of such a paradox is breaking a promise to someone in order to give pleasure to a third party. Most defenders of utilitarianism seem to be rule utilitarians, and most would probably agree that rules may be broken only in very exceptional circumstances.

More needs to be said about the rules which may be cited. Obviously, a utilitarian chooses rules adherence to which will, he believes, maximize utility. Are these any different from the customs and conventions which non-utilitarians might support as having evolved or developed to become essential elements in any peaceful viable society? I think most utilitarians would agree that there is a close correspondence. Differences probably arise only in the reasons given for following the rules.

But what about breaking the rules? When are circumstances sufficiently exceptional? The utilitarian can take everything into account—the apparent net gain in utility from disappointing a promisee and pleasing a third party; the feeling of guilt from breaking a promise; the disutility caused by weakening the convention of keeping promises; and even the intrinsic badness, if any, of breaking promises. It seems to me that a utilitarian must be both a rule and an act utilitarian, and when there is a conflict he must decide on utilitarian grounds! This is consistent with there being some rules which must never be broken. Finally, there are a great many decisions that have to be taken where no rule, custom, or convention applies: while utilitarianism provides a universal principle. The upshot is that a utilitarian must be a universal utilitarian: of course he takes the value of rules into account.

---

[4] By the economist Roy Harrod. See R.F. Harrod (1936).

Some philosophers would claim that some rights cannot be over-ridden. They are lexicographically superior to any amount of utility—for instance, no amount of good can justify condemning an innocent person to death or even prison. This has also been expressed as 'rights are trumps'.[5] Rights according to Nozick may be regarded as side contraints on actions contemplated to achieve or maximize some end.[6] If all rights to life, liberty, and property were taken to be constraints, there would be little left of utilitarianism for the state. As we have seen, governments could not adopt redistributive policies. There would also be little left of welfare economics, for almost no project or policy change can be envisaged which would not harm someone. However, it is possible that there are some wrongs which must never be permitted: with such limited side constraints consequentialism in general, and utilitarianism in particular, are viable.

I believe all this adds up to a rather solid defence of consequentialism and utilitarianism. R.M. Hare, for long a staunch defender of utilitarianism, seems to claim that the Kantian canon of universalizability implies utilitarianism.[7] This surely goes too far. One may believe that a certain act is right for oneself in given circumstances and that anyone in the same circumstances should act similarly. But why does this have anything to do with utilitarianism? A non-utilitarian may believe that some act is right, for example, suicide, in certain circumstances even though it reduces total utility: and believe that anyone is justified in committing suicide in the same circumstances.[8]

We have not touched on the main reason why most people would find strict utilitarianism unacceptable as a principle of individual morality. It requires that everyone should count equally when assessing the happiness of the community. But it would surely be not merely unnatural but immoral for a mother to care as much for a stranger as for her own child. However, rule utilitarianism may come to the rescue here. Thus a rule that parents should exercise special care for their children may be justified on grounds of social utility. As against this, a preference for friends and relatives does not in general make a convincing social rule: indeed,

---

[5] R. Dworkin (1977).   [6] Nozick (1974), pp. 30–3.
[7] R.M. Hare, *Moral Thinking*, chs 5 and 6.   [8] See P. Pettit (1987).

nepotism is condemned as undermining social utility, at least in Western countries.

Be that as it may, it does not affect utilitarianism as a principle of government, which is our main concern. One can believe that every individual's welfare should have the same weight in the state's calculations, while also respecting and supporting a moral code that allows individuals to favour relatives and friends in certain circumstances: a concern for family values is a common component of state rhetoric. I do not think there is any contradiction in this.

The mention of children and families reminds us that we have yet to consider the value of life. There has long been a debate among utilitarians as to whether the proper aim is to maximize total or average utility. Other functions of utility are also possible aims.[9] If the population remains unchanged there is no difference. Nor is there a problem if no individual or government knowingly takes decisions that affect the number of people. But both do, and so we turn to consider the problem.

UTILITY AND THE VALUE OF LIFE

Most theoretical discussion of the value of life, and practical use of the concept in decision-making, has used a utilitarian framework. We shall see whether utilitarianism seems to be as useful when population changes as when it is stationary.

We first consider individual problems before turning to those involving the state. There may be some persons who believe they have a duty to try to have a child (in certain circumstances), and that any consequentialist calculation would be inappropriate or even immoral. Others may simply not think about the matter. But if some use even a rudimentary cost-benefit analysis they will consider the net benefit to themselves and to any children they already have. But what about the welfare of the putative child? When it is born it will surely have its own utility: but that will not be counted in most people's calculations.

Classical or total utilitarians whose goal is to maximize total utility would not agree. Nevertheless, it seems to be widely accepted that there is no value in creating a new person apart from the value

[9] Blackorby and Donaldson (1984).

Table 5.1.[10] *(utils)*

	X	Y	Z
A	1	3	n
B	2	n	n
C	3	n	1
D	n	n	2
E	n	1	3
F	n	2	n

to those already in existence. This intuition may be formalized by adopting the principle that when two different situations with different populations are compared, one is better or worse than the other only if it is better or worse for those people who exist in both situations. This is called the *constituency principle*. It can lead to contradictions when betterness is judged from the point of view of different constituencies. This is illustrated in Table 5.1.

The rows are states of affairs and X, Y, and Z are persons. All other persons are equally well-off in the six different states, and can therefore be ignored. The numbers stand for levels of utility, 1 being lowest. n indicates non-existence. Thus in State A only X and Y exist with utility levels of 1 and 3. X is the only person common to A, B, and C: and Z is the only person common to C, D, and E. It is easy to see that $E > D > C > B > A$ where $>$ means more utility or better than. F is also better than E, and therefore by transitivity better than A. But A is better than F by the constituency principle, which is a contradiction.

There is an important difference between assessing the goodness of different populations without concern as to how they come about, and asking whether a move from one to another is to be recommended. Suppose that we interpret the constituency principle as a recommendation to move (a so-called deontic interpretation). There would be a continuous circular movement, as in the voting paradox. But now let us introduce the constraint that no one may be killed. All movements from A, C, and E are now forbidden and one of these states must end as the one chosen, depending where one starts from. Moreover, there is nothing to choose between them

---

[10] Table 5.1 is a simplified version of Example 3 in Broome (1999), p. 231.

according to the principle of anonymity, which states that the number and levels of well-being determine the goodness of a state of affairs regardless of who gets which level.

The above problem is very similar to that posed in welfare economics by the Kaldor/Hicks criterion. The gainers from a move from A to B could compensate the losers, but once in the B situation the gainers from a move from B to A could also compensate the losers. If potential compensation were the criterion of betterness then there is a contradiction. If it is regarded as a recommendation to move, we need a contraint to prevent the chaos of shuttling to and fro.[11] With the constituency principle a constraint that no one should be killed similarly prevents chaos.

The constituency principle certainly has to be amended when it comes to destroying rather than creating life. The person whose killing is under discussion does not exist after death. Therefore, on the constituency principle, his or her utility does not count. So the tiresome person who gives only pain to others should be eliminated. There are various ways of trying to avoid this conclusion, which most people find unacceptable. One is to abandon the constituency principle; but this is not enough, for the tiresome person may not get much enjoyment out of life, and therefore including his or her utility may not tip the balance. I think a better way is to accept the side constraint on both utilitarianism and the constituency principle that homicide can never be justified. The constituency principle may then be retained, as I believe it is in official cost-benefit calculations of the cost of death, in which the loss of utility of the deceased is not counted, only the welfare costs to survivors.

Another problem, sometimes faced by doctors, is which of two persons to let die when medical resources are not available to save both. In recent years a measure called QALYS (quality adjusted life years) has been used. The number of extra years of life is estimated for each person. How these years are adjusted for quality I do not know, but I guess that capability is the main consideration—will the person be able to function well, that is, read, write, walk, drive a car, etc.[12] It might be that one person was old and the other a

---

[11] See Little (1957), ch. 6. I introduced a second criterion—a distributional judgement—to eliminate the contradiction and chaos of shuttling.

[12] A.K. Sen defines capability as a set of such functionings, and considers it to be a better maximand than utility, although it is unclear how different functionings are to be weighted. See Sen (1982) and subsequent essays.

young woman. Should the calculation include the utility of all the children and further descendants that the young woman is likely to have? Most people will probably agree with the practice of excluding them, in accordance with the view that there is no value in creating lives. But, once again, total utilitarians must disagree.

THE STATE AND POPULATION POLICY

It may seem from the above discussion that individuals take rather a short-term view, but recent concern about global warming suggests the opposite. The difference may be that global warming can hurt people who will exist anyway. Be that as it may, governments are increasingly expected to be concerned about the consequences of present behaviour for the welfare of future generations, far into the future. This includes concern for the environment, savings, and investment: indeed there is much, often loose, talk about 'sustainability'. But the size of future generations is surely also relevant, and so the government must be concerned about the number of present births.

However, it can be argued that a woman should be free to have as many or as few children as she chooses, and that the state has no right to interfere.[13] The main counter-argument is that children may have negative externalities: that is, an extra child may reduce the welfare of others outside the family, whom the parents will not consider. This will normally be the case if non-human resources are scarce (though positive externalities are possible).

The great majority of economists and demographers are convinced that there are too many births in most poor countries for the welfare of this and future generations. At one time some developing country governments thought that Western anti-natalist propaganda was 'neo-colonial', even where the rate of population growth exceeded three per cent per annum, and national income per head was stagnant or even falling. The sheer size of the population was regarded by these rulers as a measure of the country's and their own importance. At last this attitude seems to have

[13] There is a moral problem concerning what constitutes interference and coercion. Making a second child illegal is clearly coercive. But what about taxation that heavily discriminates against second and further children? This is a general problem with all paternalist policies. We have no answer where to draw the line, which may vary according to the freedom that is interfered with.

become less common. At the other anti-natalist extreme is China where draconian methods have been adopted to reduce births. Almost all countries now support family planning even if only half-heartedly. A few, notably Singapore, are alarmed at the prospect of a fall in population, and are taking steps to encourage births.

The welfare of future generations will depend not only on their size but also on the amount of preceding investment. But we shall discuss population policy and investment for the future separately. This is fairly legitimate since investment policy will probably have little effect on future numbers of people (a possibly serious exception is considered in the section on saving for the future), and the principles governing investment are independent of the number of people and its growth.

Classical utilitarians were in no doubt about population policy. Maximizing total utility implied that the utility of a new person should count, and therefore a new person should be created so long as his life did not detract more from the utility of others than his own life contributed. With the population explosion of the second half of the twentieth century this doctrine fell out of favour. It was felt that the pursuit of total utility might lead to huge populations at a very low standard of living.

Derek Parfit refutes total utilitarianism by suggesting that it leads to the 'repugnant' conclusion that a world with countless billions of persons existing at a level that is only just bearable could be better than one with a few billions at a far higher standard of living.[14] It is difficult to imagine Parfit's teeming world. Indefinitely adding people without reducing the level of living below subsistence implies that natural resources remain abundant, in which case there is no clear reason why these people should be so poor. But Parfit argues that it is imaginable, and that an imaginary world is good enough for his refutation. In a real world, maximizing total utility does not entail very low levels for individuals. Therefore, total utilitarians might reply to Parfit that their doctrine applies to the kind of world that happens to exist and that people, with total utility maximized, would lead lives that were in no way repugnant.

A common rival aim is to maximize average utility, and many economists implicitly assume that this should be the goal. This

---

[14] D. Parfit (1984), p. 388.

clearly allows fewer births. Thus suppose a previous population of 10 each had 10 utils, and that a new person would have 9.5 and reduce everyone to that level. Then total utility rises and the average falls.

A knockdown objection to the average principle is that average utility might be increased by killing people: so it can be defended only with the side contraint that killing is not allowed. The average principle is not the same as the constituency principle, for a birth that would raise the average would be counted. But it is paradoxical that the value of a birth depends on the average welfare of others (it conflicts with the separability requirement of utility theory). The constituency principle evades this objection by assigning no value to births. But, as we have seen, the constituency principle, like the average principle, requires an embargo on killing. On balance the constituency principle seems preferable, but in practice little difference would be likely to result from following one rather than the other.

John Broome argues that utilitarianism goes wrong when assessing the value of different populations. Utilitarianism simply adds the utilities attaching to different time-slices of personhood: thus the utility of a life is the sum of the utilities of each moment. We have already noticed the difficulty that a fluctuating fortune may not have the same value as a constant one, although the sum of the years' utilities is the same. In the present context utilitarianism gives the same value to two short lives as to one long one, if the sums of the annual utilities are equal. This, Broome says, is obviously wrong.[15] I do not see why! Compare two constant equal populations, one with a life expectancy of 100 and the other of 50 years. One has twice as many annual births and deaths as the other. The pains and pleasures of births and deaths for others can be allowed for in a utilitarian calculation: and so could the probably greater amount of death expectancy in the shorter-lived population. What is obviously better about the relatively senile set?

Indifference between the senior and junior populations in the above example is consistent with preferring to extend a life rather than create a new one. This consistency stems from the difference we have already remarked on; that between assessing the goodness of different populations without regard to how they come about,

[15] John Broome (1999), p. 221.

and asking whether a move from one to the other is desirable. The constituency principle approves a policy of prolonging life while discouraging births.

Derek Parfit[16] and John Broome[17] have surveyed at length various suggested ways of valuing different and often non-overlapping populations without coming up with one that they regard as consistent (not leading to contradictions) and morally acceptable. This situation is not as distressing as it might be, because governments do not and could not think in the highly abstract manner of these philosophers. In particular, they will not compare two different populations neither of which includes existing people. They will always be comparing overlapping populations where existing people gain or lose by a movement from one to the other. Everyone has had some contact with at least two generations; most have contact with three, and some with four or even five. The next generation is thus an amorphous concept.

Certainly governments, especially in less-developed countries, do think in terms of encouraging savings and investment, to promote growth in the national income for the sake of both present and future people, and of how much money, if any, they should spend on encouraging contraception. But the degrees of freedom that they enjoy are too few, and the uncertainties of the consequences of policies too great, for any deep analysis or fine tuning. To take an example, the government of India is convinced that the population is growing too fast, that the present amount of poverty is distressing, and that more investment could reduce poverty in the future. Encouraging family planning costs little, but more investment and more relief of poverty now seem to be competitive: in this dilemma of whether to help today's or tomorrow's poor no guidance is given by comparing distant non-overlapping populations.

---

[16] In Parfit (1984). A notable contribution is his insistence that one policy now rather than another will totally change the population existing in 200 years' time. So one is not considering whether some change of policy will harm or benefit a given population in 200 years. One is arguing about whether one population is better or worse than another with no common members, and neither has common members with the existing population. For some people this may make such comparisons of less moral importance than if the changing welfare of a given population were in question. This is an example of the 'non-identity problem' as Parfitt terms it.

[17] Broome (1992, 1999).

WHAT CONSTITUENCY NOW?—ON CITIZENS AND FOREIGNERS

The state has a duty to protect its citizens. It is also generally accepted that it should protect those who legally enter its territory. The controversial issue is, of course, how far it should control and limit entry, if at all.

A total utilitarian would require the state to maximize utility in the world at large, every human being counting for one. We have already argued that probably no one would accept this, since everyone would want to give more weight to those close to him than to strangers. He may still accept that the state should give equal weight to all citizens, but is unlikely to accept that foreigners should also count equally.

An immigrant may increase or reduce the welfare of existing citizens. If he reduces it, most people will see this as a good reason for disallowing entry, or at least limiting it. If this attitude is unqualified it amounts to treating foreigners purely instrumentally, contravening Kant's widely acclaimed categorical imperative—that persons must never be treated purely as instruments. Most people would probably admit exceptions, when the potential immigrant would suffer severely, perhaps being shot or tortured, if forced to return to where he came from. Some limited respect for a foreigner's life and liberty is thus shown. But that the migrant would be better-off if admitted is not regarded as a good reason.

Communitarians presumably believe that giving the welfare of foreigners no weight, or less weight than citizens, is justified when there is a threat to community values. They believe that a common heritage, customs, and beliefs, give citizens a duty to value their fellow countrymen and their lifestyles more highly than others: and that governments have a duty to defend these values, which large-scale immigration may threaten. These arguments are most convincing when the population of the state is homogeneous. Community values are the values of some community, and most states include more than one community, and some many. Most liberals would, almost by definition, insist that the state should give equal weight to different internal communities, although many members of each community will value themselves more highly than those of other communities. These 'national liberal' and community values are consistent with a weighted utilitarianism, under which foreigners count for very little, except when their ill-fare is distressing.

Such a nationalistic attitude must distress those whose liberalism has a global dimension. If utilitarians, they will argue that every person and every institution should aim to maximize global utility: if they take a rights-dominated point of view they will argue that every human being has an absolute right to go where he will. This 'global liberalism' is very attractive to some, but very few will accept its implications.

The behaviour of states towards migration comes very close to what we believe to be the 'national liberal' attitude of most people. Migrants come in rather freely if they are wealthy and will pay taxes, or are very talented and can be expected to contribute more than they consume. But all states now prevent entry, if they can, of large numbers of poor immigrants: they would probably make the state's own poor worse-off, and if too numerous would not assimilate, and would be likely to create ethnic or communal problems.

But what of international aid? Is this not an example of some public concern for poor foreigners? Governments do not generally argue as if it were. Aid is often, if unconvincingly, defended on grounds of self-interest. But there is, admittedly, a small constituency for aid. However, it is very small, and aid given is correspondingly a tiny proportion of the national income of the rich countries. The response to appeals when there is some disaster is largely the result of television causing a temporary reduction in the great social distance that normally separates well-off viewers from the victims of disaster in some poor country. It is to be noted that aid has been requested by representatives of developing countries in the name of the state, using the idea of distributive justice between states. States do not have utility, and the discussion of interstate justice and morality is more appropriately discussed in Chapter 6.

THE STATE AND SAVING FOR THE FUTURE

As we have seen, future generations can probably be too numerous for their own good. But their welfare will also depend on prior savings and investment, and the quality of the environment that they inherit. In what follows, investment is always taken to include the conservation of assets for the future.

Savings and investment, and the rate of interest, are closely bound up with each other. When an investment project that will produce commodities in the future is being considered, the value of the sales will be discounted by the rate of interest in any conventional cost-benefit analysis. This is because by not consuming something now one can get more of it in the future. One can invest the money saved at the going rate of interest, and later buy more of any commodity than one denied oneself in the first place. If one did not discount the future value there would be no limit to the extent to which it would be rational to reduce one's present consumption!

The basic reason why one can get more of anything in the future by saving is that savings are invested, and investment is productive. To maximize production it follows that the discount rate to use is the marginal productivity of investment. Investments are then made until the net discounted benefits of the marginal investment add up to zero. Discounting is essential for rational decision-making about savings and investment, both in total and in detail.[18]

The above is a productivity reason for discounting. But it may still be asked why from a welfare point of view future commodities should be worth less than present ones. The answer is that they will be worth less if they produce less welfare, and that this will be the case if average consumption per head will be higher (assuming a diminishing marginal utility of consumption). The expected rate of growth of consumption per head multiplied by the income elasticity of the marginal utility of consumption is defined as the *consumption rate of interest* (CRI). The marginal productivity of investment is the *accounting rate of interest* (ARI).[19] The two may diverge, in which case the higher rate should be preferred until the two are brought together by increasing investment. A zero rate of interest would be best for maximizing welfare only if there was so much investment that its marginal productivity had fallen to zero,

---

[18] Non-economists often think that discounting at the going rate of interest biases choice against slow-maturing investments, such as in forestry. A tree does not grow at more than, say, 4 per cent per annum so if the rate of interest is 5 per cent they argue that no trees could be commercially planted. They forget that the price of timber may rise. There are other more difficult and interesting problems concerning the rate of exploitation of resources the total amount of which is fixed. But the simple criterion of sustainability is surely nonsensical: no use of a finite resource—any mineral—is sustainable. But these problems take one beyond the scope of an introductory book.   [19] See Little and Mirrlees *ibid.* esp. ch. 14.

and at the same time consumption per head was not expected to rise.

There can be a wide divergence of opinion about the elasticity of the marginal utility of consumption: in other words how fast the utility of a little more consumption falls as the level rises. Recent surveys of happiness suggest that it falls rapidly after a certain moderate level of real income is reached. The faster it falls the stronger is the utilitarian argument for redistributing income from the rich to the poor. An egalitarian will tend to select a high value—in other words a high CRI. Yet some egalitarians are concerned that we may be neglecting future generations and believe discounting is wrong. It can only be that they somehow cannot believe that, despite the growth of the past 500 years, given the rate at which we consume natural resources, and pollute the atmosphere, future people are likely to be richer than us. An expected fall in average consumption would imply that savings and investment should be subsidized. But those most concerned about the future are probably looking to the distant future, and fearing catastrophe for at least some of the human race. They would, I think, want a major reorientation of investment so as not to increase welfare in the near future, but to reduce the risk of more distant catastrophe.

We have seen that discounting the value of future commodities does not bias outcomes against future people. Future utility is not thereby discounted. We argued earlier that most people would put a lower weight on the utility of remote people than of those close to them, and even that it would be immoral not to do so. But no one today can be more remote than those who will be born in, say, 200 years time. So many people think that less weight should be given to their utility. However, one may nevertheless believe that governments should give as much weight to the welfare of future people as to that of those already existing.

6

Utilitarianism, Justice, and Equality

Around 1970 a wave of attacks was mounted on consequentialism in general and utilitarianism in particular. The main ground of attack was no longer that interpersonal comparisons were unscientific or impossible. Utilitarianism was accused of lack of respect for individuals. John Rawls wrote 'utilitarianism does not take take seriously the distinction between persons': this was because he tendentiously described the process of estimating social utility as one of 'conflating all persons into one through the imaginative acts of the impartial sympathetic observer'.[1] To maximize total utility one must compare the marginal utility of transferable resources to different persons: the distinction between persons is all important. It is only the utilitarian theory that resources should be equalized which requires the assumption that people are much the same, and this is not an essential part of utilitarianism.[2] However, utilitarianism was also attacked for neglecting individual rights.

A.K. Sen in several papers argues that utility is a poor measure of whatever should concern one with regard to the lives of individuals. He is particularly concerned that people may get used to deprivation, and declare themselves contented. 'As people learn to adjust to the existing horrors by the sheer necessity of uneventful survival, the horrors look less terrible in the metric of utilities'.[3] He also complains that 'a person is viewed by a utilitarian as nothing other than the place in which that valuable thing called happiness takes place'. Sen here interprets utility in a psychological sense. But a utilitarian is free to adopt an interpretation of

---

[1] John Rawls (1988), p. 19.
[2] Derek Parfit examines in depth Rawls's claim and utilitarian arguments in the light of different assumptions about the nature of personal identity in *Reasons and Persons*, ch. 15, sections 111–18.   [3] A.K. Sen (1984).

utility broader than declared contentedness or a smiling face. In short, one can both accept the importance of Sen's concerns and still be a utilitarian.

UTILITARIANISM AND EQUALITY

However, the main criticism of utilitarianism was that it ignored equality. Concern for equality has two main elements. One is that people should be treated with equal concern unless there is a moral reason for discrimination. The other is that people should have equal welfare, unless their lesser welfare is their own choice or fault, or benefits them absolutely.

Strict utilitarianism is hardly to be faulted on the first ground, for everyone's welfare is to count the same. Indeed utilitarianism is too egalitarian for almost everyone's taste, as we saw in Chapter 5. It is also quite surprising, at least for someone of my generation, that utilitarianism should be attacked on the second ground. In accordance with the doctrine of diminishing marginal utility of income it required that wealth should be taken from the rich and given to the poor until marginal utilities were equalized. At this point total utility would be maximized. This seemed to be embarrassingly egalitarian. Moreover, it is historically true that utilitarianism was the main intellectual force driving most equalizing social reforms of the nineteenth and twentieth centuries.

However, this equalizing tendency of utilitarianism depends on people being equally good converters of money or other resources into utility. If some handicapped person is a very feeble converter, then his marginal utility of income may be very low, equal perhaps to that of a millionaire, when his income is only a few thousand a year. It is also possible for a rich man to be a poor converter. If someone is born with expensive tastes he needs more money than other people to achieve the same level of utility, and his marginal utility of income may remain high even at a high income level. His tastes are a handicap, but most people will feel little sympathy for him. They will envy his consumption of cigars, champagne, and caviar: and envy is often taken by philosophers as a measure of inequality.

So equalizing marginal utility does not leave everyone equally well-off. But before utilitarianism is condemned two defences should be considered. First, it is probable that most people are equally good converters, or nearly so: and other moral systems, as we shall see, also fail to deal with exceptions; indeed exceptions by definition cannot be covered by general principles. Second, it is not obvious that one should go further than equalizing marginal utility when dealing with handicapped persons. In particular, A.K. Sen's *weak equity axiom* is unacceptable. It reads: 'let person i have a lower level of welfare than person j for each level of individual income. Then, in distributing a given total of income among n individuals including i and j, the optimal solution must give i a higher level of income than j'.[4] This implies transferring income from everyone with higher welfare to one with lower welfare even if it makes no difference to the latter. It also implies giving more income to the man with expensive tastes. This is not to say that it would always be wrong to reduce one person's welfare in order to make a smaller addition to that of another. One would, however, want to know the details of the case.[5]

RAWLS'S THEORY OF JUSTICE

Dissatisfaction with utilitarianism, mainly on the ground of neglecting equality, led to attempts to create systems of political principles based on contract or equality. Much the most comprehensive and important of these is that of John Rawls. His published work began in 1958 but it acquired very wide attention only with the publication of his book *A Theory of Justice* (1971). We shall refer to the revised edition (1990). This work has been an extraordinary phenomenon. It received great acclaim in non-academic periodicals, partly because it dealt explicitly with substantive moral issues after many years of meta-ethics, and partly because it seemed to be very egalitarian. Many philosophers also treated it with enormous respect. Brian Barry described it as 'a work of major importance... of great significance for moral and political philosophy',[6] before demolishing every one of its main supports. Robert Nozick similarly wrote 'Political philosophers now must either work within Rawls's theory or explain why not', before explaining why not.[7] Every one of the 14 authors in *Reading Rawls* dissents in some

---

[4] A.K. Sen (1973), pp. 18–20.

[5] There have been attacks on utilitarianism on grounds other than its neglect of equality, by prominent philosophers, notably Bernard Williams, Alasdair MacIntyre, and T.M. Scanlon, which we neglect at this point in the argument.

[6] Barry (1973), 'Apologia'.   [7] Nozick (1974), pp. 183–231.

important respect.[8] Subsequent criticism has continued, leaving, it seems to me, the theory in ruins. Nevertheless, one must agree that it is an important work: in its 500 pages almost every moral and political issue is fully discussed with great understanding. One must also agree with Nozick, and so we must first outline the theory, and then explain 'why not'. We cannot do more than give the highlights in this short introduction.

Rawls believes that what is good comes from what is right, not vice versa as is the case with all teleological theories. His theory is supposed to be a contract theory. From the contract are derived the principles of justice which should govern the constitution, institutions, laws, and procedures of the state. The so-called contract is made between people who choose from behind a 'veil of ignorance'. They are very ignorant. They do not know the state of development of the society of which they will be members. They do not know their own capabilities or tastes. They are rational and self-interested, which means that they want to further their own conception of the good, but they do not know what that conception is. They have no known substantial moral beliefs so that the principles of justice they choose are the result only of rational individual self-interest. They have no idea what their position in society will be.

These initial conditions are, of course, designed to make these wraith-like delegates impartial: they cannot further their own interests since they do not know what they are. An impartial observer or judge has been an important component of many philosophers' theories. Rawls's embellishment of the idea of impartiality by the 'veil of ignorance' is not original. It was, as we have seen (page 6), introduced by Harsanyi in 1953: but Harsanyi drew very different utilitarian conclusions from those of Rawls, which are more original. Rawls's delegates are constrained to be unanimous, which implies that there is no meaningful contract. However, they agree on a set of principles of justice which should determine the basic structure of society. These are (see *A Theory of Justice*, p. 266):

1. Each person is to have an equal right to the most extensive total system of equal basic liberties compatible with a similar system of liberty for all.

---

[8] Norman Daniels (ed.), (1975).

2. Social and economic inequalities are to be arranged so that they are both:
   (a) to the greatest benefit of the least advantaged, consistent with the just savings principle, and
   (b) attached to offices and positions open to all under conditions of fair equality of opportunity.

The first part of the second principle has come to be known as the difference principle. It is also known as the maximin principle: that is, compare the worst possible outcomes in different states, and then choose the state with the best of these.

In addition to the two main principles there are two priority rules. Only one need concern us. It says that the first principle has lexicographic priority. This means that no increase in benefit under the second principle can compensate for the slightest loss of liberty. But Rawls later qualifies this: lexicographic priority takes charge only when a certain level of economic development is reached. In extremely poor societies some liberty may be sacrificed for economic benefit.

Benefit and advantage under the second principle are measured in 'primary goods', which are the 'things that every rational man is presumed to want' (*ibid.* p. 54). They include rights, liberties, opportunities, income, and wealth (social goods), as well as natural abilities such as health and intelligence.

We cannot do justice either to Rawls's deep defences of these principles, or to the range and strength of attacks upon them. We can deal only with a few of what seem to be the most important criticisms, which we group under three headings, (a) the original position, (b) primary goods, and (c) the difference or maximin principle.[9]

The first and most fundamental criticism is that Rawls has not succeeded in showing that the principles that would be chosen from behind the veil of ignorance are principles of justice. Those that Rawls claims would be chosen do not seem to accord with one's intuitive ideas of justice. Thus there is no mention of entitlements or deserts. This dissonance may be due to some disagreement about what justice means, and we discuss the concept of

---

[9] We do not consider the very surprising lexicographic priority rule, because in fact Rawls relaxes it with results that are too complicated to pursue (see Barry *ibid.* ch. 7).

justice in the following section. There is also no reason to suppose that real people would approve or feel bound to obey a state founded on Rawls's principles.[10] Rawls has not surmounted the basic weakness of any contract theory.

Rawls adopts 'primary goods' as a measure of being least advantaged and of benefit. These goods are mostly instruments, that is, things not wanted for their own sake. They are incommensurable except in terms of their value for some end. But Rawls cannot thus value them for that would be utilitarian. Rawls seems to think in terms of a representative member of the most disadvantaged group. It remains obscure how someone or some group is to be judged more or less disadvantaged than another. Ironically, Rawls's reluctance to go behind primary goods to needs or wants implies that no regard can be paid to the needs or wants of the most disadvantaged, that is, handicapped people. We have seen that utilitarianism has been denounced for this failing: Rawlsianism is as bad or worse.[11] Most economists discussing Rawls tend to assume that primary goods are just wealth, and nothing seems to be lost by this assumption.

We finally turn to the difference or maximin principle, which has excited the most criticism. Dimly observing all possible societies from behind the veil of ignorance, anyone or everyone would, it is assumed, choose that society in which the most disadvantaged group fared best, regardless of the situation of the rest. Rawls thought it sufficient for this choice that anyone might be a member of this group. Nothing is known of the relative size of the group (which in a random process determines the probability of being a member) or its relative poverty.

The absurdity of maximin can be made clear by an example. Compare two possible societies in both of which the most disadvantaged group is one per cent of the population. Society A's most disadvantaged group has an income per head of 100, and the average income of the rest of Society A is 400. The income of the most disadvantaged group is 99 in Society B, where the average income of the rest of the population is 500. Rawls's person in the original position opts for A. There is a one per cent chance of his gaining 1,

[10] See Little (1980).

[11] Barry strongly criticizes Rawls for this reason, see *ibid.* chs 5 and 6. He also strongly criticizes the international implication of Rawls's principles (*ibid.* ch. 12). See also Little (*ibid.*).

and a 99 per cent chance of his losing 100, as compared with B. Only the most incredibly risk-averse person could make this choice.

Rawls would not accept the relevance of such an example. He lays it down that persons behind the veil of ignorance have no knowledge of the probability of their being a member of any most disadvantaged group (and therefore of the relative size of this group in each country), and indeed that they have no knowledge of their own attitude to risk. He thereby removes almost all basis for rational choice. All that is known of the societies between which the choice must be made is the wealth per head of their most disadvantaged groups. But in choosing the society with the best-off such group (and the difference between the best and the next best must be known, and may be very small), the *possibility* that there is a high probability of a very large gain foregone must be known. It makes no sense to claim that persons in the original position do not know their attitude to risk: by their very choice they proclaim themselves to be infinitely risk-averse.

The utilitarian analysis of choice under uncertainty wins hands down. If the chooser is risk-neutral he maximizes the expectation of utility. Degrees of risk aversion or attraction can be incorporated, but not the infinite risk aversion required by maximin. Rawls has an aversion to trade-offs, as shown by the lexicographic priorities of his principles. Maximin also proclaims an aversion to trading risk against reward.

THE MEANING OF JUSTICE

The concept of justice has been traditionally concerned with rights and duties: with giving a person his due, and not infringing his rights (except possibly for good moral reasons). This is generally known as procedural justice. It is very different from Rawls's concept of 'social' justice, which is defined as follows: 'A conception of social justice, then, is to be regarded as providing in the first instance a standard whereby the distributive aspects of the basic structure of society are to be assessed'.[12] Social justice is also conceived of as fairness, as implied by the title of Rawls's earlier essay 'Justice as Fairness'.[13] This is because his principles of justice are, he claims, the result of an

---

[12] *A Theory of Justice* (revised edition), p. 8.
[13] *The Philosophical Review*, Vol. 57 (1958).

impartial agreement or bargain, in an initial situation designed to ensure that no representative's interest can be favoured at the expense of another's.[14] Actually, the representatives are so stripped of qualities that they may be thought of as identical, indeed as a single person, in which case 'agreement' and 'bargaining' are otiose. Impartiality, however, remains as the salient condition of fairness.

Social justice has become a favourite expression used to promote a strong interventionist and redistributive role for the state. Writers in this relatively recent tradition describe outcomes or states of affairs as just or unjust. Conflicts then arise between procedures and outcomes, and it has been argued that one cannot know whether a procedure is just without assessing its consequences. It is claimed, for instance, that it is socially unjust that a person is very poor through no fault of his own, and that government intervention to supply his needs is therefore socially just. But to tax others to aid him infringes their property rights, which is an injustice. Since property rights are an indispensable element in any viable social order we end up by saying that a government must confiscate property which is socially unjust in order to be socially just.

A very similar contradiction arises with positive discrimination. It is said to be socially unjust that a certain class of persons has more difficulty in achieving some standard of performance (required for entrance to a college, or for a degree, or a job). Positive discrimination lowers the standard for this class of persons. But this is manifestly unfair (unjust) on others who achieve a higher standard and see less qualified persons preferred to them. These contradictions arise only from an extension of the application of 'justice' to situations where it was not previously held to be appropriate. We are not arguing here about substance, only about words or concepts. We have already argued that there is a moral case for taking away someone's property to help a person in need. But this is not a matter of justice. Rather, it is a case for letting welfare override justice. One may also approve of some positive discrimination without asserting that it is just. However, those who want to promote certain public policies may not be willing to give up the use of the persuasive power of the concept of social justice in the interests of clarity.[15]

---

[14] *A Theory of Justice* (revised edition), p. 11.

[15] I am not, of course, claiming that those who write under the banner of 'social justice' have nothing worth saying. For instance, David Miller's *Principles of Social Justice* contains valuable discussions of needs, deserts, and equality.

We need to say more about justice, and its branches. Distinctions are made between commutative and distributive justice, and between procedural and substantive justice. Anthony de Jasay prefers *suum cuique* (unto each his own) which he attributes to Cicero, and 'to each according to...' (which he attributes to Louis Blanc who originated in 1839 the precept 'to each according to his needs, from each according to his abilities') as better reflecting two types of situation in which justice is a pertinent consideration.[16] 'Unto each his own' depends on what is a person's own. Ownership includes the liberty to do anything that is not rendered unacceptable by restricting the liberties or rights of others or by breaking a social convention whose function is to protect such liberties. Breaking a contract is unacceptable because it infringes the right of the promisee to fulfilment. Material and intellectual property is, of course, included: and a person is free to use his property subject to the same provisos. We have already discussed property and other rights (pp. 29–38). Justice in this category consists of protecting liberties together with the enforcement of contracts and certain social conventions.

An important feature of Jasay's treatment is to link the importance of liberty as a foundation stone of justice to epistemology rather than to some ethical intuition: that is, to the distinction between verifiability and falsifiability. Liberty to do something cannot be easily verified, because the list of things one can do is limitless. But a liberty claim can be falsified in a limited number of ways, such as causing harm to others or infringing their rights. There must therefore be a presumption of liberty.[17] This is very similar to the presumption of innocence as an essential principle of criminal justice.

DISTRIBUTIVE JUSTICE

As Jasay says, 'the vast bulk of the world's goods, tangible and intangible, is produced and distributed as a matter of course as and when liberties are exercised and mutually agreed obligations are discharged'.[18] What then is left? Duties that are not also obligations

---

[16] In what follows I rely heavily on Jasay's penetrating article 'Justice' in *The New Palgrave Dictionary of Economics and the Law*, Macmillan, London, 1998.

[17] For a contrary opinion see J. Raz *The Morality of Freedom*, pp. 8–14.

[18] *Ibid.* p. 19.

have not been discussed. These consist of the duties of those in authority, including parents, teachers, employers, judges, officers, and civil servants, as well as the government, to behave in an appropriate way towards those, including animals, over whom they exercise some authority. These are cases in which there is no contract (although sometimes an implicit contract is claimed), so that the person in authority has not conferred a right giving rise to a corresponding obligation. Exercising these duties involves some distribution of benefits or burdens, or both. There is then a distributor and something to be distributed. The distribution or redistribution may be the main purpose of some action or policy. But very often it is incidental to some need to regulate or adjudicate. A distributional effect is thus often an unavoidable accompaniment of an exercise of authority.

So there is a distributor and something to be distributed, including burdens as well as benefits. Is there a presumption of equal shares? This question arises only when there is a divisible amount of benefit or burden to be given to a number of eligible claimants. It makes sense in the case of a mother, cutting up the cake at the children's party. But one does not want to give all criminals the same sentence, all pupils the same marks, and so on. Thus 'to (or from) each according to . . .' takes over, where the ellipsis stands for some criterion such as desert, need, guilt, or prowess of some kind. The general principle of 'treat like cases alike, and unlike differently' is almost vacuous, because there is almost always some respect in which cases are like, and some respect in which they differ. But if no morally relevant criterion is found to differentiate the cases, then there is a presumption of equality: but clearly this depends on the value judgement that there is no morally relevant decisive criterion.

A special case of 'to each according to' is 'to each according to his contribution'. In cases of economic production with more than one participant a measure of contribution is the marginal product of each participant. With perfect competition workers will receive their marginal products. This was given a normative interpretation by J. B. Clark who described it as fair.[19] Thenceforth, for about three quarters of a century it became impossible for a theorist who constructed a model with an equation of wages and marginal products

[19] J.B. Clark (1885).

to escape being accused, in certain places, of being a capitalist lackey. We have already seen in Chapter 3 that a perfectly competitive economy may be far from optimal in any moral sense, and that therefore equating wages and marginal products does not imply that the author is proposing the moral rectitude of this equation.[20]

Distributional problems also arise when there are fewer indivisible goods than eligible claimants (those who pass some agreed qualifying test). There is not enough to go round. This is a very common situation, arising, for instance, in the case of jobs and entries to universities. The circumstances vary greatly. Rules, precedents, conventions, and customs give rise to legitimate expectations. Deserts and merit play a large part. But it seems impossible to generalize, and quite often there may be no consensus as to what is fair.

Kidneys for transplant is a favourite example of the problem of how to distribute indivisible goods. The following dilemma shows the contrast between utility seeking and fairness very sharply. There are two cases of severe kidney failure and only one replacement kidney available. One patient is young and otherwise healthy: giving him the kidney would raise his expectation of life by 50 years. The other patient is older, and his expectation of life would be raised by only 10 years. According to the Qalys criterion (see Chapter 5) there is no doubt. The younger person gets the kidney. But is this fair? If the judgement of greater expected utility if the kidney is given to the young person is not morally decisive, then there is a presumption of equal treatment. The only equality possible is giving the two patients an equal chance of having the transplant. So toss a coin! Often, tossing a coin is the fairest method of deciding. But we have already argued that sometimes it may be morally right to override justice and fairness.[21] What would you do—favour the young person or toss a coin?

The state cannot abstain from distributional judgements. Even a mini-state must raise taxes to provide for the maintenance of law and order, and defence; and it must make appointments to official positions. Indeed almost anything it does will have distributional

---

[20] On all this, see Schumpeter (1954), pp. 869–70.
[21] It is interesting that in ordinary parlance the word 'just' is seldom applied to distributional outcomes; the word 'fair' is normally used, at least in English. I believe that in some languages 'just' and 'fair' are synonymous.

consequences, and in the case of a welfare state the distribution of benefits becomes a major issue. But the state is not responsible for distributing everything as Rawls implicitly assumed. The reasoning behind this preposterous notion seems to be that the whole national product is a result of cooperative activity, and is therefore collectively owned. A person's salary is a handout from the state, and its size is to be determined by the Rawlsian principles of justice that we have discussed.

INTERSTATE DISTRIBUTIVE JUSTICE

We saw in Chapter 5 that some developing countries have demanded aid in the name of interstate distributive justice. We have argued that justice and other moral concepts make sense only within a society; and we have further argued that distributive justice within a state is a concern only when the state, or some subordinate authority, has some benefits or damages to distribute. We have thus argued that taking resources from the rich for the sole purpose of assisting the poor is not just although it may be morally desirable, and a feature of good societies.

What then can interstate distributive justice mean? It is clear that, to some extent, a society of states exists, and that many claims to interstate justice are both made and recognized. Most of such interstate justice is concerned with sovereignty, with the right to conduct wars claimed to be just, with equality of treatment in international institutions, with the interpretation and observation of treaties, and so on. This is what is generally called commutative justice. However, problems of distribution arise when there are costs and benefits from the use of a resource, such as a river, which is common to more than one country. When an agreement is reached it can be presumed that all the common users gain (unless participation is forced by threat of war); but some may gain more than others. There is usually no supra-national government to regulate such agreements in the name of justice, although elements of such a government are coming into being in Europe. Trade, including capital movements, is the most general example of international activity. But the gains from trade do not accrue to any world distributor; where trade is regulated by treaty under an authority such as the World Trade Organization, it is commutative not distributive justice that is involved. Within a state many would argue that reasonable equality of persons is a moral desideratum. But reasonable equality of states would be an absurd aim. How could China and Chile be equal?[22] This is not to say that wealthy people and the governments of wealthy countries should not try to help the poor in poor countries.

DWORKIN AND EQUALIZING RESOURCES

Like Rawls, Ronald Dworkin has tried to construct a coherent and convincing set of principles, defining good government, that centre round the idea of equality. Indeed, he shows more detailed concern for equality than Rawls; but he is similarly concerned only with public political principles, not with personal morality.

Equality of what? In his early work, Dworkin pronounced equality of respect and concern to be the basic principle. In his most recent work on which I rely in the rest of this section he has wisely dropped respect.[23] How could anyone, any government, treat everyone with equal respect? What more operational principles or policies does Dworkin derive from the abstract notion of equal concern?

He begins by disagreeing with utilitarianism, and more generally with the idea that what governments should promote is equality of welfare. He rightly says that utility has various interpretations. We agree in finding fault with interpretations that include political and other impersonal preferences. We interpret personal utility as an ordering of the choices made by rational well-informed, self-interested persons of different bundles of economic goods, and we deem this to be a measure of economic welfare (see Chapters 1 and 2).

We have already discussed interpersonal welfare comparisons, but it is necessary to bring them into sharper focus when considering whether inequality, somehow defined, is a good reason for some redistribution of income or assets. Interpreting utility as subjective well-being makes sense when considering changes in a person's utility. Thus we can reasonably suppose that a rise in someone's real income increases his well-being, other things being

---

[22] For a more extended discussion of this issue, see Little (1980).

[23] R. Dworkin, *Sovereign Virtue, the Theory and Practice of Equality* (2000). The original version of chs 1 and 2, with which we are here mainly concerned, come from *Philosophy and Public Affairs*, 10, 1981.

equal. But can we sensibly argue that we should transfer income or wealth from A to B whenever A's economic well-being, or happiness, is greater than that of B? Under utilitarianism this would follow only if the transfer would make more difference to B than to A. This is getting more sensible but would seem shocking to many people. Act utilitarianism makes no reference to how inequalities arise and can certainly be faulted on this score. We shall consider later whether rule or indirect utilitarianism can be similarly faulted.

According to Dworkin, an inequality that results from a person's own deliberate choice should not be compensated or taxed away. Those inequalities that result from the inheritance of material resources or income-enhancing genes, or sheer 'brute' luck should be eliminated so far as possible.[24] This is a principle which may be widely acceptable. Dworkin seeks to define equality of *resources* in such a way as to implement this principle better than equality of welfare.

What is wrong with equalizing welfare? Consider first those who are handicapped. Dworkin is worried that a possibly hopeless endeavour to raise their welfare to, say, the average level would result in excessive resources being transferred to them: he is also worried that the impossibility of such an endeavour would in practice lead to an inadequate transfer.

The handicapped are poor converters of resources into welfare, but so also are those with expensive tastes. But Dworkin does not think that the latter should be compensated, because he holds that people must be held responsible for their preferences. However, an exception would be someone who has a craving that he regrets but cannot overcome. Some may dislike the idea that drug addicts or paedophiles should be compensated for any loss of welfare that their craving may cause them. But humanitarian considerations may sometimes overrule this dislike.

Some people are very good converters, such as those to whom Sen has drawn attention, who are contented, even happy, with very little. They have not chosen their humble situation but have become content with it. A poor peasant woman whose life and functionings are very limited is an example. This paradoxically

---

[24] Winning or losing from insurance or betting is random luck. Suffering from an uninsurable accident is 'brute' luck.

presents a very similar problem to that of the handicapped. Trying to make such a person happier or more capable may be frustrated by her low marginal utility, which is the result of the culture of her society, and maybe her husband. This has been called the case of 'the tamed housewife'.[25]

Before considering Dworkin's claim that equalizing resources is a better objective than equalizing welfare, let us briefly examine the strength of these objections to equalizing welfare. First, it seems to me that utilitarianism can handle the problem of the handicapped not perhaps well, but as well as can be. The difficulty of comparing marginal utilities is as likely to give them too little as too much, and too much as too little. The problem of expensive tastes may seem more difficult for act utilitarianism but the indirect version can, as so often, come to the rescue. It is reasonable to regard people as at least partly responsible for their tastes, for example, whether to start smoking tobacco or cannabis; and they can with difficulty usually change them. Since expensive tastes (and smoking is surely one such) reduce the overall level of welfare, indirect utilitarianism requires them to be discouraged. Smokers should not be compensated for the high tax on tobacco! Rule utilitarianism can also easily cope with the idle welfare addict.

We turn to equalizing resources. In theory, transferable resources are no problem. Give everyone equal purchasing power, and let them bid for all non-human resources, and subsequently trade. A Pareto-optimum is attained. It is non-transferable human resources—abilities and disabilities—that are the problem. Dworkin claims that (hypothetical) insurance markets can overcome the problem. Everyone can use some of his purchasing power to buy insurance against becoming disabled (the incidence of disabilities can be assumed to be known). Inequalities of ability are more difficult. Dworkin assumes that persons behind his (thin) veil of ignorance know their own abilities, but do not know what value they will prove to have in the real market that eventuates. The insurance market offers them insurance against their income falling below some level which they stipulate. Premiums would be paid from actual incomes and could with advantage to all parties be assessed as an increasing proportion of such incomes. These premiums are the analogue of taxes, which would be used to

[25] J. Roemer (1996), ch. 7.

compensate those whose income fell below the level which they had chosen to insure. This very imaginative piece of social science fiction is intended to justify progressive taxation and welfare benefits by being notionally based on rational choices that people would make behind a veil of ignorance. (This veil is, however, much thinner than that of Rawls, that is, the veiled participants are more knowing.) Dworkin's story sounds like a way of trying to ensure equality of opportunity. But he is adamant that he does not agree with what he calls 'starting gate' theories. When the race gets under way, inequalities grow. People must be allowed to retain the gains from savings, hard work, and the use of their differing talents. Outcomes should be 'ambition sensitive' but not 'endowment sensitive'. But inequality of material resources must not be allowed to develop! To do full justice to both principles is impossible, and so a compromise is required. Dworkin makes the somewhat unoriginal suggestion of an income tax as a compromise. But his hypothetical insurance market does not tell us how progressive the income tax should be. Understandably he also favours high death duties or inheritance taxes.

Dworkin does not provide a satisfactory solution of the problems he explores. It is not obvious that the amount the average person would pay for insurance against polio, say, is a good measure of the disability benefit a sufferer should receive (also the degree of disablement varies, which would be difficult to specify in an insurance policy). Insuring against a low income is more dubious still, quite apart from the severe moral hazard involved. Roemer provides a convincing argument.[26] If A has superior talents in every respect compared to B, so that A can expect to have a higher income than B whatever the value of his talents turns out to be, there seems to be no reason to suppose that insurance would equalize the effect of such a difference of talents. More generally, how does one judge when the advantages and disadvantages of differing talents have been fully compensated? The answer must be when resources are equal in some other dimension which can only be some conception of welfare.[27]

To try to answer the question 'equality of what?' evidently gets one into very deep water. The aim of Dworkin and others has been to equalize people only in respect of circumstances for which they

<hr />

[26] J.E. Roemer (1986).   [27] *Ibid.* p. 25.

are not themselves responsible. But responsibility is itself highly debatable. Dworkin thinks that people must be considered to be responsible for their preferences (except in the case of cravings that they would rather be without). This can be challenged. For instance, the 'tamed housewife' is not compensated. Attempts have been made to improve on Dworkin's delineation of responsibility. Important recent contributions to the extensive debate include those of R. Arneson, G.A. Cohen, and T. Scanlon. The issues are fully discussed by Roemer in *Theories of Distributive Justice* where full references can be found (up to 1996). The search for a morally convincing account of responsibility, covering all circumstances, has, it is perhaps needless to say, resulted in no agreement.

THE MEASUREMENT OF EQUALITY

Suppose next that we assume away all moral problems involved in treating personal welfare as the goal which society should seek to equalize. We are not out of the wood, for the government clearly needs to know when one vector of welfares is more equal than another. We need a measure of welfare equality. As soon as we are considering more than two persons, there is a problem (ignored by Dworkin).

In Table 6.1, which row shows the most equal distribution? It is not obvious. If equality of welfare is a goal of society, it must be presumed that a more equal distribution is better for society than a less equal one. In that case, we have to combine the individual welfares (or incomes) of the table, to make a total of social welfare. Equality is then instrumental, and may have no independent value. This is the theory supporting Atkinson's famous measure of equality of *incomes*.[28] His index of equality is 'the proportion of the present total income that would be required to achieve the same level of social welfare as at present if incomes were equally distributed'. The smaller the proportion the less equal is the distribution. Calculating this index requires a SWF relating a person's income to the contribution it makes to social welfare. The more concave the function (that is, the more rapidly the marginal contribution to social welfare falls as income rises) the greater is the index of inequality (that is, one minus the index of equality, which ranges from 0 to 1).

[28] A.B. Atkinson (1970).

Politics and Philosophy

Table 6.1.

	Persons		
	90	80	10
Welfare	100	60	20
	115	40	25

The Atkinson index is liked by theoretical economists because greater equality of income entails greater total utility (provided that total income remains unchanged). It seems basically utilitarian, although the function relating income to social welfare could incorporate a concern for equality itself. However, it is not much used in practice, because the required welfare function embodies a value judgement, which a positive economist, seeking to compare 'objectively' the equality of income distribution between countries or over time, is loth to employ.

To the extent that it links equality to social welfare, the Atkinson measure is disliked by those egalitarians who insist that the value of equality is not, or not mainly, instrumental. Equality is valuable in itself, and need have no direct relation to social welfare.[29] It is not easy for such an egalitarian, or anyone, to choose between any of the purely statistical measures of the inequality of a list of numbers, such as the range or the variance. They will choose, one supposes, according to what the numbers stand for, and which of the features of inequality, that their intuition tells them is most undesirable, is given most weight by the various measures. Those fascinated by these intricacies should consult Temkin,[30] or Sen.[31] We shall refer only to the Gini coefficient, which is the most used.[32] For a given population and national income the denominator of the coefficient

---

[29] This and many other egalitarian views are exhaustively explored with great clarity in Larry S. Temkin, *Inequality* (1993).

[30] *Ibid.* ch. 5.   [31] A.K. Sen (1972).

[32] The actual formula is

$$\frac{1}{2}\sum_{i=1}^{i=n}\sum_{j=1}^{j=n}\frac{|y_i - y_j|}{m^2 n}$$

where y_i and y_j are the incomes of the ith and jth persons, n is the number of persons, and m is the mean income.

is given: so inequality is measured by the numerator which is simply the sum of all the differences in incomes. The intuition is that the badness of a distribution is the sum of the distances by which anyone's income is less than that of anyone else. Some might think that this measures the total amount of envy in society; but this is not very plausible since a person does not compare himself with every other person in any large community.

We should note at this point that income may be a poor measure of a person's welfare, or of the narrower concept of his standard of living, or indeed of his use of resources or expenditure. A person may be very rich in assets that yield little or no income. He may live on capital or capital gains. Wealth is thus in principle a better measure of the extent to which one person is better-off than another, in respect of either welfare or resources. However, human wealth has to be included. It can, in theory, be measured as the present discounted value of potential future earnings (including pensions), but this calculation is clearly not very objective. All of the above is well-known to economists, investors, and tax inspectors; but philosophers sometimes seem to be unaware of the problem. Throughout this book we refer either to income or to wealth as an indicator of material welfare. In principle we always mean wealth, but often write 'income' because it is a more familiar concept to most people.

Finally, we note that some egalitarians do not accept the Pareto principle that one situation cannot be better (worse) than another if no one is better-off (or worse-off). In particular, some may believe that it would be a social improvement if the rich were levelled down, even without any gain to those poorer. Here one must be clear whether one is referring to incomes (or wealth), or to welfare. If a rich person's expenditure directly reduces the welfare of someone poorer (without reducing his income or wealth) then levelling down does make someone better-off, and there is no conflict with the Pareto principle. A SWF can allow for such external effects; these, incidentally, may also be positive, as when one enjoys the sight of a Ferrari, or gets some consumer's surplus from visiting a stately home. However, an extreme egalitarian may believe that society would be better if the rich were less rich even with no gain in welfare for anyone. Other egalitarians believe that inequality would be increased if a society was simply scaled up, with twice as many people and resources of all kinds. Would there not then also be twice as much inequality? Yes, numbers count, says Temkin.[33] If they count for utility they should count for inequality. A scaled-up society has more utility and more inequality. Where does that leave us? My view is that numbers should not count for either utility or inequality.

Finally, comparisons may be made between generations and between countries. When one is thus comparing different populations, measures of inequality lose most of their rationale. The Atkinson measure depends on a hypothetical redistribution within a community at a point in time. Also, a comparison of inequality in, say, England now with Victorian times, or with Japan, cannot reasonably invoke the simple idea of its being bad that one person should be worse-off than another through no fault of his own, or of envy. However, it is possible that inequality of whatever, devoid of normative interest, could help to explain other features of society. If so, one would simply select the measure with the most explanatory power.

SUMMARY

We began by considering utilitarianism and equality. We turned to the idea of equality as a principle to govern the basic design of society, and examined Rawls's *A Theory of Justice*. We concluded that his principles were unacceptable. However, it can be argued that Rawls's maximin principle has little to do with equality: for all that matters are the primary goods (a mixture of resources and capabilities) enjoyed by the most disadvantaged group in society. It has been reasonably argued that someone holding such views is a humanitarian not an egalitarian.[34]

We next briefly discussed international justice, arguing that there are as yet no principles of interstate distributive justice. But this does not imply that the governments of rich countries should not be concerned to try to help the poor of the world, difficult though that is.

We then turned to Dworkin who, more than anyone, has claimed that equality should be a guiding principle of government. He claims 'Equal concern is the sovereign virtue of political community'. This is a great rhetorical statement. But is it any less vacuous

---

[33] *Ibid*. ch. 7.   [34] For example, Temkin *ibid*. p. 8.

than 'like cases should be treated alike'? Dworkin proceeds to argue that equal concern requires that the government should aim to equalize resources, defined in such a way that people's situations are equalized only in respect of circumstances for which they are not themselves responsible. Unfortunately, Dworkin's suggested methods of equalizing resources are, we found, unconvincing.

Dworkin does not consider how it is judged when one state of society is more equal than another, a judgement that is essential if equality is to be a guiding light for government actions and policies. We found no measure of equality, whether of income, wealth or welfare, to be generally acceptable.

One need not conclude that egalitarians are pursuing a chimera. The reformer may well exclaim 'for goodness sake, we often know when a government's policies will, broadly speaking, produce more or less equality'. Equality of what? Wealth, income or welfare? Broadly speaking again, it does not matter which; and any measure of it will do, for all measures will agree in most circumstances. But one may, nevertheless, conclude that the difficulties are such as to make equality a poor target which can divert attention from what matters most, such as the welfare of the very poor, and how best to deal with difficult cases where the responsibility of the sufferer is unclear, and where the success of any measure of relief is uncertain.

7

Contractarianism

What is contractarianism? Originally it referred to the theory that states could, in principle, have been created by contract. Recently, the word has come to be used much more loosely. It now refers also to the creation of moral codes, or 'social contracts' by agreement; and even the agreement has been whittled away almost to vanishing point.

We have already discussed Rawls, and Harsanyi (1953), who are sometimes classed as contractarians. However, there has been a new outcrop in recent years based partly on the Theory of Games. We take Gauthier and Binmore as examples. Our account is superficial, since even a glance at elementary game theory is reserved for Part III. Thus the reader at this point may be able to understand only the outline of the argument; but we hope that this will suffice for some understanding of these authors' contributions. We also refer to the views of T.M. Scanlon who describes himself as a contractarian.

David Gauthier is the most prominent advocate of the view that morality derives from agreement.[1] He is anti-utilitarian because maximizing welfare may involve a redistribution of revenues which infringes rights and creates free-riders and parasites (those who shift their costs onto others, like poor cuckoos who lack the capability of building nests). He is basically a libertarian, like Nozick. His anti-utilitarianism is thus very different from that of Rawls or Dworkin: they do not think that people are entitled to the fruits of talents that are a matter of genetic luck and thus belong to society. Gauthier would view any redistribution of these fruits as unjust. In his own words, 'A utilitarian society lacks any substantive aim but is concerned to realize the greatest sum of individual goods.

---

[1] D. Gauthier, *Morals by Agreement*. He draws attention to K. Baier *The Moral Point of View: Rational Basis of Ethics*, and G.R. Grice *The Grounds of Moral Judgement*, as earlier advocates of similar theories.

A just society is concerned only to enable each person to realize the greatest amount of her own good, on terms acceptable to all'.[2]

He distinguishes two kinds of utility maximizers, those who pursue their own interests regardless of others, and those who realize that there is a possibility of benefit if they cooperate with others. These latter realize that cooperation may require some constraint on their own behaviour. They are called *constrained maximizers* if they have some disposition to cooperate. Productive cooperation requires a division of the extra output that results from cooperation. This is a bargaining problem, for which Gauthier claims there is a determinate rational solution, given that the cooperators are constrained maximizers who can also recognize each other as such. His solution to the problem can be, and has been, challenged since there can be different views as to what is rational on the part of each cooperator. But let us suppose that a solution is found such that no participant believes he can gain by breaking the bargain arrived at.[3] The bargains are thus self-policing: they require no external constraint from moral precept or the law. This enables Gauthier to argue that morality itself derives from the constraints required for productive cooperation.

Not all productive activity requires cooperation. Gauthier points to the economic concept of perfect competition, according to which each trader maximizes utility given the prices of commodities which neither he nor any other trader can influence. Since no cooperation is required, Gauthier declares this to be a morality-free zone. 'Morality arises from market failure'.[4] This is a mistake. Every transaction that is not simultaneous requires trust. When two people go to exchange a pear for an apple one normally profers his fruit first. More seriously, all credit and future transactions are by definition non-simultaneous. The market would be a strange place without trust. This, however, is not a serious flaw in Gauthier's thesis: his argument is not weakened by admitting that all trade is cooperative.

Gauthier recognizes that viable bargains between those with unequal endowments may be regarded as unfair. He, therefore, incorporates a Nozickian proviso requiring that a person's endowments have been acquired without reducing the welfare of

---

[2] *Ibid.* p. 341.   [3] In game theory this is known as a Nash equilibrium.
[4] *Ibid.* p. 84.

anyone with whom he had cooperated.[5] This proviso, which also
governs current exchanges, raises several problems. It must be
derivable from reason alone, incorporating no moral injunction,
otherwise Gauthier's main thesis is undermined. He recognizes
this, and claims that all constrained maximizers would accept the
proviso. This is arguable. Other doubts arise about the fairness of
Gauthier's solutions. Limiting the proviso to cooperative transactions, must, in the opinion of those who emphasize distributive justice, reduce or negate its value. Thus the proviso does not operate
in the case of invaders occupying land if they have no dealings
with existing natives. The neglect of a serious discussion of restitution, or compensation for unjust aquisition of property, will also
excite the same critics.[6] The logic of Gauthier's position is that fairness and justice are ideas that can apply only to cooperating persons and their arrangements. This may be acceptable, but not that
all morality springs from agreement, so that one cannot have moral
duties towards those with whom one does not happen to deal, or
with whom cooperation is impossible, because of, say, their mental
incapacity. We shall return to the thesis of morals by agreement
after examining some other contractual views.

Recently, K. Binmore has published an enormous work on moral
and political philosophy with a strong game theoretic basis. His
two volumes run to nearly 900 pages and include over 200 figures
(including subdivisions).[7] It is not a reader-friendly work, with frequent backward and forward references, and repetition; it requires
much previous or concomitant study of game theory, which is hard
work for the unpractised reader of mathematical texts. However, it
is replete with discerning analysis and challenging judgement. I
am not confident that I can give a fair outline of Binmore's work in
a page or so, but here goes.

Binmore has one great hero, Hume, and three *bêtes noirs*, Plato,
Kant, and Gauthier. Plato is a fascist. Kant is a metaphysician.
Gauthier does not play game theory properly. Binmore objects to
the idea of a constrained maximizer with a disposition to cooperate, and especially to the idea that constrained maximizers can
often recognize each other. The contestants in game theory games

---

[5] *Ibid.* p. 192.   [6] For example, Brian Barry (1995), pp. 42–5.
[7] K. Binmore, *Game Theory and the Social Contract*: Vol 1, *Playing Fair* (1994); Vol. 2,
Just Playing (1998).

can communicate only through the moves they make. They are like ideal bridge players who describe their hands only by bids, and not at all by frowns, tones of voice, or how they hold their cards. Binmore also objects to Gauthier's solution to the bargaining problem; but Gauthier claims that with acceptable assumptions his solution is compatible with the most highly regarded bargaining theory.[8] In my opinion it is not an objection to the concept of constrained maximization that it is anathema to game theorists. Common sense surely suggests both that it may be rational to behave so as to invite cooperation, and that this is recognizable by others. Admittedly, this implies an expectation of further games. Whether such behaviour and recognition is wholly independent of morality is another matter.

Binmore is a contractarian of a special kind. He regards the social contract as the whole set of all commonly understood coordinating conventions. The social contract coordinates behaviour to produce an equilibrium in what he calls the *game of life*: it is claimed to be self-enforcing because it is in the interest of every citizen to obey the rules provided enough others do the same (Vol. 2, p. 5). These conventions are also regarded as 'fairness norms' (Vol. 2, p. 470), and they have evolved over time, probably from food-sharing agreements in hunter-gatherer societies. They are moral rules that bind only by habit or custom (Vol. 2, p. 145). He calls them theories of *the seemly*; they neither presuppose the good as in consequentialist theories, nor rights that must be respected regardless of consequences.

The game of morals is played when a change of some contract is under consideration. Here Binmore uses the device of a veil of ignorance. But his veil is much thinner than that of Rawls. The participants are Adam and Eve, and the original position is the status quo in the Garden of Eden. Adam and Eve come together to negotiate a contract to divide the gains from marriage. The veil drops. They still know everything except who they are. They have personal preferences, but also empathetic preferences. This means that each can form preferences such as 'I would rather be Adam with X than Eve with Y' where X and Y can be thought of as shares

---

[8] These intricacies are discussed in the contributions of Binmore and Gauthier to David Gauthier and Robert Sugden (eds), *Rationality, Justice and the Social Contract* (1993).

of the gains. Empathetic preferences permit comparison of Adam and Eve's utils. The bargain arrived at is not binding when the veil is lifted. Either can demand that the veil again descends for a new negotiation. Equilibrium is reached only when neither demands renegotiation.

As I understand it, the game theory determining the solutions is that of an infinitely repeated non-cooperative game. I am not competent to discuss the details. But the upshot is an egalitarian division of the increased utility arising from cooperation, which Binmore claims is very similar to that which Rawls would reach with maximin, although Binmore does not deal with primary goods. I confess I do not understand how Binmore arrives at this result. Dare one say that Binmore and Gauthier have a lot in common? Both are concerned to expound a theory of morals by agreement. Both see viable contracts as fair divisions of the advantages to be gained by cooperation. Both distance themselves from utilitarianism, and from natural rights, although Binmore concedes that utilitarianism would make sense with a powerful, benign, and paternalistic government. Gauthier tries to support the fairness of his contracts and his initial position with his proviso. Binmore's initial position is the status quo, and there is no proviso. He seems to believe that over time the status quo will become fairer, that is more mutually agreeable.

We turn to the contractualist arguments of T.M. Scanlon. His basic principle is that 'An act is wrong if its performance under the circumstances would be disallowed by any system of rules for the general regulation of behaviour which no one could reasonably reject as a basis for informed, unforced general agreement'.[9]

Scanlon is acclaimed by Brian Barry as correctly conveying the idea of impartiality which is an essential feature of moral principles.[10] Thus Scanlon writes 'If I believe that a certain principle P could not reasonably be rejected as a basis for informed unforced general agreement, then I must believe not only that it is something which it would be reasonable for me to accept but something which it would be reasonable for others to accept as well, in so far as we are all seeking a ground for general agreement. Accordingly, I must

---

[9] T.M. Scanlon, 'Contractualism and Utilitarianism' in Sen and Williams (eds), 1982. A more recent development and elaboration of Scanlon's contractual theory is *What We Owe to Eachother* (2000). 					[10] B. Barry *ibid*. p. 110.

believe that I would have reason to accept P no matter which social position I were to occupy'.[11]

This sounds like choosing behind a veil of ignorance, but it is not. Scanlon is writing about real people who are trying to reach a general agreement governing social behaviour and social institutions. Harsanyi and Rawls were writing about a single rational spirit designing Utopia. Scanlon maintains that they wrongly assumed that they were capturing the idea of impartiality. He distances himself from their principles, while believing that utilitarian solutions could on occasion be generally agreed.

The veil of ignorance is quite troublesome. Its thickness varies greatly from author to author. When it is lifted are the erstwhile identical participants, now becoming real different people, committed? If so, it is doubtful whether the solution is just. If not, all hell may break loose. Rawls himself is concerned that the state, resulting from his principles, should be stable; but a concern for stability apparently constrains the deliberations of the veiled participant in a manner not obviously consonant with his maximin logic.[12]

The problem can be brought into sharp focus by confronting the average utilitarian solution of Harsanyi with actual inequality of resources. A veiled expected utility maximizer opts for maximum average utility. The marginal utility of everyone is made equal, to the extent possible, by shifting resources. But some remain worse-off than others, since some people are better than others at converting resources into welfare. However, if such an economy were realized the worse-off might claim a renegotiation in the manner of Binmore. But if the veil were again lowered the same inequality would result. The less well-off must give up, or try to find some other way of reaching agreement, which may or may not be possible.

Scanlon ends the article quoted by denying that morality is merely a device for mutual protection, as some philosophers have urged. The desire for protection is important because it determines what can reasonably be agreed. 'But the idea of general agreement does not arise as a means of securing protection. It is in a more fundamental sense what morality is about'.[13] In his recent book[14] Scanlon changes the motivation that people are assumed to have for trying to reach agreement from desire to reason. He also clearly

---

[11] Scanlon *ibid*. p. 121.   [12] Little (1978), p. 40.   [13] *Ibid*. p. 128.
[14] Scanlon (1998).

states that his theory is about a large part of morality, not all of it. Some behaviour may be wrong, for instance some forms of sexual activity, although a principle that permitted it could not reasonably be rejected by others seeking general agreement. This is why his book is called *What We Owe to Eachother* since this well describes the limited domain of his theory.

Before leaving the subject of contractualism, we must consider the views of Robert Sugden, who argues that the 'contractarian enterprise' is impossible.[15] He describes this enterprise as that of deriving principles of morality by analysing the problem that would be faced by rational individuals in a state of nature. They would agree, it is claimed, to certain rules of cooperation and restraint. Moreover, these rules would need to be impartial, or universalizable: and it is this that makes them rules of morality. I think that all the authors considered in this chapter, except perhaps Binmore, were pursuing this enterprise, albeit in different ways.

Sugden's dismissal of the enterprise is simple. He denies that bargaining problems have uniquely rational solutions.[16] Furthermore, rational solutions may not be impartial, and thus have a claim to be called moral. It is possible for customs and conventions to be established and to be self-policing, so that it would be irrational for anyone to challenge them; and yet some such conventions may be partial and, in the opinion of many, immoral. Feminists will surely agree. It should be noted that Sugden strongly supports the view that customs and conventions have evolved as essential features of society, and that some have acquired moral status. He denies only that such moral codes can be justified by appeals to reason.[17]

Let me suggest some conclusions of my own concerning contractarianism. We must distinguish different varieties. The early contractarians, Hobbes and Locke, were writing about real people in a state of nature forming a contract to create a state. Moral

[15] Robert Sugden, 'The Contractarian Enterprise', and 'Rationality and Impartiality: Is the contractarian enterprise possible?', both in David Gauthier and Robert Sugden (eds), *Rationality, Justice and the Social Contract* (1993).

[16] See also Robert Sugden, 'Rational Choice: A Survey of Contributions from Economics and Philosophy', *Economic Journal*, Vol. 101, Number 407, July 1991.

[17] R. Sugden (1986).

concepts and rules were prior to the state. There was no question of moral codes, or most of them, being created by agreement. This idea is a contribution only of recent contractarians. In Hobbes's theory the state was fully authoritarian. But with Locke the people were principals and the state their agent. How principals can best control, and get the best out of agents, has become a much-studied branch of economics. Whether this study has anything to offer to the theory of the modern state will be considered in Part III.

Harsanyi and Rawls have been classed as contractarians. This is not really correct. We have seen that Rawls's 'contractors' are really one, and one does not contract with oneself. With Harsanyi (1953), the veil of ignorance was there to establish an empathetic member of society (or an outside observer) who makes impartial moral judgements that are uncontaminated by knowledge of his position in society and his personal preferences. With neither author is there any question of morality being created by agreement. We now concentrate on those authors who claim that it can be—Gauthier, Binmore, and Scanlon, and no doubt others we have neglected.

Morals by agreement is an attractive thesis. In examining it, it is important to distinguish between whether the claim is that morality is being explained, or justified. Let us first consider the former lesser claim.

It is surely true that conventions and customs have a long history and can be at least partly explained in evolutionary terms. If they are generally agreed by nearly all rational well-informed people, and are regarded as important for a secure and thriving social life, then it is also understandable that they acquire moral force. This statement, however, calls for some elaboration. A convention is a rule of behaviour such that almost everyone conforms, provided almost everyone else conforms, which they all expect. They are not enforced by any authority, and are effectively self-policing (although there may be occasional queue jumpers). Nothing has been said about agreement or contract.

In some circumstances when all members of a well-defined group benefit from following some convention, there may be said to be an implicit contract, which the members are obliged to follow. But generally there is no *obligation* to conform to a convention. However, to say that a convention acquires moral force is to say that people believe that they ought to conform, in other words have a duty to conform. Only a few conventions, such as those of respect for persons and property, do acquire moral force. Conventions such as saying 'please' and 'thank you' are part of the cement of society, but are regarded as a matter of manners not morals.[18]

Thus the desire to live together in a viable peaceful society has given rise to a host of conventions, some of which are so important that they are believed to be a matter of morals. But these conventions are not like agreements to divide the spoils of cooperation, the gains from trade, as hypothesized by Rawls, Gauthier, and Binmore. Conventions against homicide do not result from bargaining about the division of the increased production that results; and moral virtues such as kindness are not always productive.

Morality by convention thus seems to me to be a more inclusive explanation of the growth of moral codes than morality by agreement. However, conventions that spring from coordinating social interaction are not themselves plausibly related to all areas of morality, such as one's duty to one's children, or parents. Finally, it is important to note that the theory does not seek to justify all the moral conventions that have developed. Some of them may not be defensible and may change. In any case, one is as free to criticize the moral codes of one's own society, as of any other society.

Some contractualists, especially Rawls and Gauthier, seek to justify the morality that they claim to be derivable from agreements that are supposedly rational. They regard the rationality as a necessary basis for fairness. We have argued that morality by convention cannot explain all morality, and that what it does explain is not neccessarily good. Morality by agreement explains less, since moral codes stem more from conventions than from agreements: and its claim to justify those moral codes which it can explain, by reference to the rationality of such agreements, is not convincing.

Our recent contractualists do not spell out the implications of their theories for the desirable extent and forms of government. As we saw, Gauthier's views tend to be libertarian, but this stems more from his emphasis on rights than from the theory of morals by agreement. Binmore describes himself as a Whig, and tends to approve of equality, if only in the long run. Scanlon is even less

---

[18] We cannot do full justice to the subject of conventions. The classic work is D.K. Lewis (1969): see also R. Sugden (1986, 1998).

commital. However, one can say that the more problems of coord-ination can be, and are in practice, efficiently solved by unforced agreement, the less need there is of government at all levels. The degree to which reliance can and should be placed on such con-ventions and agreements is both an empirical and a moral problem which is further discussed in Part III.

8

Communitarianism

Communitarianism is radically different from any of the strands of political philosophy that we have as yet examined. These have all accepted that everything good is reducible to what is good for persons, and that a state derives its legitimacy solely from individual concerns and decisions.

Communitarians will have none of this.[1] Their objection to any philosophy based either on individual rights or needs is that a person does not exist independently of the society of which he is a member. Concepts such as deserts or justice have meaning only in the context of a particular community. In neglecting persons' deserts, their history and their attachments, philosophers such as Rawls and Nozick fail to understand justice. Furthermore there are goods, such as patriotism, which are irreducible to personal costs or benefits.[2]

It is true that persons are virtually unimaginable except in a social context. Their abilities and goals, their plans, their pains, and their pleasures, are relative to other persons, and are formed or experienced in, and are deeply influenced by, the communities to which they belong (or have belonged). However, this does not imply that their plans and actions are wholly determined. The individualistic approach to morality and social welfare requires that persons are autonomous. There is free will. However strong the influence of the community, a person remains free to choose between many options. He can have rights, and may or may not deserve what he gets. He may also question the rules and conventions of society. Indeed, he may question his own values, and is not constituted by his ends.[3]

---

[1] Among recent philosophers, the communitarian case has been most fully argued by M. Sandel (1982).

[2] See especially Charles Taylor (1995), ch. 7.

[3] For a counter view, see Sandel (1982), especially pp. 55–9. Sandel's arguments are in turn effectively contested in Will Kymlicka (1990), ch. 6.

Alasdair MacIntyre is the most radical of the communitarians. He rejects, root and branch, all modern moral and political philosophy that stems from the Enlightenment, and is based on welfare or on rights.[4] There is no way of reconciling the claims of NM (Nozickian Man) and RM (Rawlsian Man). The former has worked hard, and deserves his possessions: so it is unjust to tax him to help indigent RM. But RM plausibly claims that he does not deserve his poverty, which is therefore unjust. But Rawls and Nozick both neglect deserts, and hence justice. What is or is not deserved is essentially relative to community values. 'The notion of desert is at home only in the context of a community whose primary bond is a shared understanding both of the good for man and of the good for that community and where individuals identify their primary interests with reference to those goods'.[5]

We have lost such community values. 'But our pluralist culture possesses no method of weighing, no rational criterion for deciding between claims based on legitimate entitlements against claims based on need'.[6] MacIntyre sees this predicament as a failure stemming from the Enlightenment's destruction of traditional values based on virtue. He wants a return to a philosophy to be derived from the Aristotelian concept of virtue, as propounded in the *Nicomachean Ethics*. He is disgusted with modern bureaucratic capitalism. The pretensions of managers, including I think economic planners, seem to excite his antipathy as much as greedy capitalists. What is the political bottom line? It seems to be to create small communities in which some virtues may be preserved pending the final collapse of bureaucratic capitalism.

That there are irreconcilable values, which society has (tautologically) no method of weighing against each other, is a thesis associated very much with Isaiah Berlin who did not, like MacIntyre, see it as a disaster.[7] There can be compromises, short of warfare, between parties holding irreconcilable views. The lack of an overarching morality in the light of which every issue can be rationally settled is not to be deplored.

Neither MacIntyre nor our other communitarians pay adequate attention to the reasons why many people, including myself, have

[4] I here refer to MacIntyre (1985), and not to subsequent work where he favours Aquinas.   [5] *Ibid*. p. 250.
[6] *Ibid*. p. 246.   [7] Berlin (1969), pp. 167–72.

a deep distrust of communitarianism. It seems to us that a shared understanding of the good of the community has often been a shared understanding of evil. Surely Hitler was an arch communitarian. Every dictator, every founder of a sect, appeals to communitarian values.

This is not, of course, to say that all communitarian values are to be condemned. Belonging to a community is an important element in the well-being of many people and may provide support and a beneficial focus to their lives. It may also give them status. Nationalism is the prime example. Recent history makes it clear that most members of ethnic communities will tolerate being badly, even cruelly, governed by their own people rather than be subjected to foreign rule. Neither patriotism nor nationalism can be praised or condemned unreservedly, regardless of historical, ethnic, and ideological circumstances. But we hold to the view that the good of communities and nations is reducible to that of individuals.

PART III

ECONOMICS AND POLITICS

Introduction

The absence of 'Philosophy' in the title of Part III should not be taken to imply that there is no philosophy involved in the discussions of this part. There is no attempt to justify or criticize the substance of any moral code. Only in this sense is there no philosophy. But the existence of some moral code is often presumed, and, in Chapter 9 especially, the manner in which conventions have probably grown into a moral code is discussed. In this respect, Chapter 9 may be regarded in large part as a continuation of Chapter 7.

The overlap of politics and economics is very extensive, and our coverage of it is quite limited. We concentrate on the provision of public goods, and on attempts to explain some economic policies and trends using political economy models of public choice. We also look briefly at some aberrations of the collective decision-making process—rent-seeking and corruption.

We ignore macroeconomic issues, problems of the stability of output and prices, and of the rate of growth of national income; and the role of government in achieving the most desirable outcomes in these dimensions. There is probably little or no disagreement with the view that governments have a macroeconomic role to play; but much disagreement on how best to play it, in terms of both institutional design and delegation, and direct action by way of fiscal, monetary, and exchange rate intervention. Serious discussion of these difficult problems requires much more economic training and experience than is required for the other issues addressed in this book. I do not feel that I can usefully engage the minds of philosophers or politicians with these problems, and therefore leave political macroeconomics to another author.

9

Games, Conventions, and Public Goods

GAMES

Game theory was invented in 1944 by Neumann and Morgenstern in their famous book *The Theory of Games and Economic Behaviour*. The most well-known games theorem, 'The Prisoners' Dilemma' was described in 1950 by A. Tucker in an unpublished paper, and John Nash defined the key concept of equilibrium in a non-cooperative game at about the same time. Interest in and development of the theory grew slowly, but has burgeoned in the past 25 years. Applications have been made, most famously perhaps in biology and defence, but increasingly also in economics and politics. However, game theory is regarded as having its roots in economics.

The subject of game theory is the analysis of best behaviour when that depends on the behaviour of one or more other people (or animals). Most social interactions are games, almost by definition of the word interaction. In economics the most obvious among many applications is to bilateral monopoly. But in this book we consider only the interface with politics. Game theory has ramified extensively, but it is fortunate that only a few twigs on a single branch need be examined for the purpose of understanding its relevance to political theory.

To the game theorist, the prisoners' dilemma must seem a very small, stale part of his subject. But at one time it was thought to constitute a crucial argument for economic planning. I can recall giving a seminar in the 1960s that must have favoured some relatively laisser-faire policy. One objector cried 'What about the Critique?' referring to my *Critique of Welfare Economics*, a book that was wrongly supposed to have been somewhat left wing. Another cried 'What about the Prisoners' Dilemma?' I knew how to answer the first critic but I probably did not know how best to deal with the second rhetorical question. I do now. But first we must explain the dilemma, which arises in a game that is played only once, a so-called *one-shot* game.

There are two players, and each has a choice between an identical pair of actions (or *stratagems* as they are known in game theory). The choices are made simultaneously. The four pairs of stratagems can be shown in a 2 × 2 matrix, as in Fig. 9.1.

We call the player who decides on the row 'Rowena' and the player who decides on the column, 'Colin'. The stratagems are labelled 'cooperate' and 'defect'. In the original story of the prisoners, 'cooperate' means 'not confess' and 'defect' means 'confess'. We use 'cooperate' and 'defect' because many games can be illustrated with such a 2 × 2 matrix, in which 'cooperate' generally stands for a non-aggressive cooperative stratagem, and 'defect' for the opposite. When Rowena and Colin have each chosen their stratagems, one of the four cells is the *outcome*. Each cell contains two numbers; the first is the reward or *pay-off* of Rowena, and the second the pay-off of Colin. The numbers stand for units of utility (utils), or for whatever the participants are deemed to be maximizing. For the purposes of the prisoners' dilemma ordinal utility is good enough: a higher number is chosen rather than a lower, and the utils are not interpersonally comparable.

The story of the prisoners' dilemma is that if both refuse to confess, each receives a light sentence and if both confess, a heavier sentence. If only one confesses, the confessor gets the light sentence or even goes free, and the other prisoner gets the heaviest sentence. In this story, for the higher number to be chosen, it must represent years of remission from a maximum sentence of, say, 10 years in prison. We can then substitute in Fig. 9.1, say, $a = 7$, $b = 2$, $c = 9$, and $d = 4$ (as in Fig. 9.2) representing 3, 8, 1, and 6 years in prison.

	Colin	
	Cooperate	Defect
Rowena Cooperate	a, a	b, c
Defect	c, b	d, d

Figure 9.1. *Utils.*

Colin

Not confess Confess

	Not confess	Confess
Not confess	7, 7	2, 9
Confess	9, 2	4, 4

Rowena

Figure 9.2. *Years of Remission.*

Now for the solution. If Rowena chooses 'confess', she gets c rather than a if Colin chooses 'not confess'; and d rather than b if Colin chooses 'confess'. If $c > a$, and $d > b$, she is better-off with 'confess', whichever Colin chooses.[1] We have chosen our numbers so that this is the case. It is easy to check that if Colin chooses 'confess' he is also better-off whichever Rowena chooses. This means that 'confess' *dominates* 'not confess' for both. So the cell Confess/Confess is chosen, and each prisoner serves six years. If only Not Confess/Not Confess could have been chosen each would have served only three years. The given ordering of the pay-offs, $c > a$, and $d > b$, is definitive of a prisoners' dilemma[1]. How could either have chosen not to confess? If one chose not to confess and the other chose to confess, the former would serve eight years, and he or she knows that the other's choice is dominated by 'confess', as is his or her own own. In the original story, the prisoners could not even communicate. But communication would not result in both refusing to confess. For even if both promised not to confess, neither could trust the other not to break his promise. Only if a *binding commitment* could be made would neither confessing be achievable. But if a binding commitment could be made then the game would be a *cooperative game*, and the prisoners' dilemma is by definition a non-cooperative game, and therefore the solution of both confessing is a tautology, true by definition.

The importance for economics of the prisoners' dilemma is that it defines a situation in which free interaction of the parties—in a so-called market—cannot achieve the best outcome. In economic jargon they cannot reach a 'Pareto-optimum', as defined and discussed in Chapter 3: in other words, there is *market failure*. Those

---

[1] If $c>a$ then $d\geq b$ is sufficient for a prisoners' dilemma: similarly $d > b$ and $c \geq a$ is sufficient.

who distrust policies of relying on 'the market' tend to believe, or anyway argue, that prisoners' dilemmas are pervasive.

We must in fairness return to Gauthier's idea explained in Chapter 7. He believed that mutual cooperation could result if the prisoners were able to recognize each other as 'constrained maximizers'. In effect, each would have been able to perceive that the other would keep his promise. Binmore aimed to shoot him down with the tautology that a prisoners' dilemma precludes cooperation. But Gauthier could still claim that mutual cooperation was achievable by rational players even in a one-shot game without any binding commitment. If the game theory definitions are accepted, then the game described would not be a prisoners' dilemma. Gauthier's theory is attractive because it is obvious that one can often discern whether people are trustworthy, and because mutual coordinating and viable agreements are frequently achievable without binding commitments, which in turn normally require an outside enforcer. However, it is important to note that Sugden, Binmore, and Scanlon (authors referred to in Chapter 7) are themselves strong believers in unforced, non-committal agreements. The difference is that they believe that such agreements come about by a repetition of games of social interaction. I think this is more plausible than that 'cooperate' might have been played by both our prisoners in what was a one-shot game.

There are various strategies whereby a repeated game can result in a cooperative equilibrium. One is Tit-for-Tat which means copying your opponent's last move. It is assumed that Tit-for-Tat players begin with 'cooperate'. If one plays 'cooperate'and meets another Tit-for-Tat player, the optimum solution of both cooperating is repeated indefinitely. It is an equilibrium provided the probability of any game being the last is sufficiently small. This is because the gain from playing 'defect' lasts for one round only, while the loss from both defecting instead of both cooperating is repeated indefinitely.

A caveat about 'indefinitely' is needed. There must not be a fixed number of games. If the number is fixed then the last game is a one-shot prisoners' dilemma with the Defect/Defect outcome. In the penultimate game also, neither player can rationally play 'cooperate' because the other loses nothing by playing 'defect' since there is no future gain from cooperation; and so on by 'backward induction' to the present. This minefield is easily avoided by

Colin

		Cooperate	Defect
Rowena	Cooperate	1, 1	0, 10
	Defect	10, 0	0, 0

Figure 9.3. *£ Sterling.*

assuming that at each round there is only a very small probability of there being no future games.

Almost everyone faces a prisoners' dilemma almost every day. Any non-simultaneous trade is a prisoners' dilemma, and virtually all trades are non-simultaneous. If Rowena hands over goods agreed to be worth £10, and Colin hands over £10, they both gain a little (say, the utility equivalent of about £1), or they would not have traded. If there were no trade there would be no gain. But if only one hands over the goods or cash, he or she gains £10 in value, as in Fig. 9.3 which shows the standard inequalities of a prisoners' dilemma.

Refusal to trade is a dominant strategy for both. But trade occurs! Are we wrong then to call any such situation a prisoners' dilemma? Is it really a cooperative game? No!, because neither party can make a firm commitment. It may be objected that to take the cash and not deliver the goods, or vice versa, is illegal. It is true that some exchanges are supported by contracts under which the cheat may be successfully sued for damages. But innumerable trades are not so supported, and depend on trust.

The mistake is to treat exchanges as one-shot prisoners' dilemmas. Everyone hopes to trade frequently, but someone who has acquired a reputation for cheating or breaking promises will find it difficult. The answer to the student who cried 'What about the Prisoners' Dilemma?' is twofold. First, one-shot prisoners' dilemmas are rare. Second, indefinitely repeated games are extremely common, and everyday experience tells us that unforced cooperative solutions are very often arrived at somehow.[2] To analyse

---

[2] A deeper analysis of why prisoners' dilemmas lend little support to the view that the state is necessary for the functioning of any society is that of Jasay, 'Prisoners' dilemma and the Theory of the State' in *The New Palgrave Dictionary of Economics and the Law.*

Colin

		Cooperate	Defect
Rowena	Cooperate	3, 3	0, 2
	Defect	2, 0	1, 1

Figure 9.4. *Utils.*

exactly how they may be reached by rational self-interested persons is a subject in game theory that may be fascinating for some. But what matters for political economy is that they *are* often reached without detailed regulation or enforcement by government.

There are other games that are not prisoners' dilemmas because there is no dominant strategy, but where some external authority or government might be needed for the best outcome to result. One such is the Assurance Game where the pay-off structure is as in Fig. 9.4.

For Rowena, cooperation is best if Colin cooperates, and defection is best if Colin defects, and vice versa. This can arise if people do not want to be free-riders or 'suckers', that is, contribute when others do not. It has been argued that traffic congestion in a city centre may be a case in point.[3] The players would like to see the centre traffic-free but no one likes the idea of being the only one with a special permit to enter, and no one is going to keep out if others do not. In some situations of this kind, externally administered rules may be needed for the best outcome. But, in others, a convention may come into being that achieves an equally good result.

CONVENTIONS

I follow Sugden in defining a convention as any stable equilibrium in a non-cooperative indefinitely repeated game that has two or more stable equilibria.[4] There is a stable equilibrium if it is in each

---

[3] Joshi, Mary S., Vijay Joshi and Roger Lamb (2001).

[4] Sugden (1986), p. 32, and (1998). Another important reference is Lewis (1965). Every more recent author also draws on Hume (1740), Book III, Part II, sections ii–v.

player's interest to follow a certain stratagem provided everyone else (or almost everyone else) follows that stratagem. Such a stratagem is a self-enforcing rule. But not all self-enforcing rules are conventions. In normal parlance a self-enforcing rule is called a convention only if one can imagine a different rule that would also be self-enforcing. A classic example is the rule 'drive on the left'. One can imagine everyone driving on the right but the convention (in the UK) is otherwise.

Conventions in society are pervasive. Language itself is a convention. It is conventional to speak English in England. It is also a matter of convention what particular words mean. The use of money is a convention. Many problems of coordination, such as who gives way to whom in various circumstances, are settled by conventions, such as 'first come first served'.

Conventions concerning property deserve further mention. We discussed the acquisition of property in Chaper 4, arguing that property was acquired legitimately by working, by gift or inheritance, and by the use of existing assets; but that original property was acquired mostly by force. However, sometimes convention is important, especially when doubts arise. Thus if ownership of something is contested, possession conventionally plays a large part, as implied by the adage that possession is nine points of the law. Another convention concerning property is that finders are keepers. Proximity may also be a deciding factor in certain circumstances.

It is clear that many social interactions are 'regulated' by convention. But many are also regulated by law. Much law is a codification of conventions, from which it evolved. This suggests that convention is not always enough. To put it another way, conventions are supposed to be self-enforcing: but thieves, muggers, and road hogs, may become alarmingly common, and call self-enforcement in question. Although some libertarians may claim that anarchy has never been given a chance, few if any would argue that no law and no police force is required.

PUBLIC GOODS

Pure public goods are classically defined by two characteristics. First, they are in *joint supply*: this means that one person cannot be supplied without supplying others, and that the consumption of the good by one person does not reduce the consumption of others. This condition is also called one of *non-rivalry*. Second, they are *non-excludable*: that is, if the good is produced no one can be excluded from enjoying it, which also implies that no one can be charged for its use.[5]

We have defined *pure* public goods: but both defining characteristics may be more or less satisfied. If a road carries little traffic an extra vehicle does not interfere with others; but when there is congestion, then (by definition) it does. Exclusion is also a matter of degree; at some cost it is usually possible to exclude people. If a road is little used the cost of exclusion per person or vehicle excluded would be high, probably exceeding the revenue from fees. The reverse is the case for busy autoroutes.

The classic examples of pure public goods are lighthouses and national defence. The fact that one rarely comes across other examples in the literature makes one wonder whether there are any! Government itself, or at least the provision of law and order, is also often given as an example. But it is not a pure public good, because use of the courts may be charged for, and police protection is sometimes bought.

An alternative definition of a public good is that people can enjoy it without paying. This also admits of degrees. A good or service may be supplied without any payment, and under the alternative definition it would then be a pure public good. Production could even be in the private sector, and yet it would be a pure public good if it were 100 per cent subsidized. But a good may be only partly subsidized. Logic then requires us to define public-ness in terms of the degree of public subsidization.

Consider the British National Health Service. Health service is very far from meeting the classic definition. One can tend and care for a person without tending or caring for others: and it is not true that greater use by some does not reduce use by others, as hospital waiting lists testify. Excludability is no problem, so that charges can be made. Yet the service is subsidized to a very high percentage of its cost, and it is almost entirely produced in the public sector. In fact, in most countries health and education constitute a very large part of public expenditure: but, apart from the traditional sector of public health (sewage, pollution, etc.), they are not classic public

---

[5] P.A. Samuelson (1954).

goods. Their subsidization is usually justified on redistributive grounds, but the redistributive element could rather easily be reproduced without public production.

In the case of education, the argument for subsidization is not only that poor people cannot afford enough. Primary education became compulsory because it was believed that some parents would not educate their children adequately, even if they could afford it. Economists call goods which, it is felt, should be subsidized because people would not otherwise consume enough, 'merit' goods. It is a kind of positive paternalism, just as making some drugs illegal is negative paternalism. But if education, up to a certain age, were to be made compulsory, then it had to be free. However, education is still not a classic public good. Parents could be given education vouchers with which they could buy education produced in the private sector: they might or might not be means tested.

The classic definition singled out goods whose cost could not be recovered by sale of the good. Where the amount to be provided is a variable (as in the case of defence), it is then very difficult to know how much to provide. In theory, the cost of, say, a marginal squadron of fighter aircraft should equal the sum of the amounts that each citizen would be willing to pay to have that squadron.[6] This is, of course, impossible to find out. So the amount spent on defence is a political issue concerning which economists have little useful to say.

We have thus far not considered the provision of public goods by subscription. It does occur. In the UK, blood is given for transfusions, and the lifeboat service is financed by subscription: in the USA, public television is similarly financed. However, these are rare instances. Much more frequent are relatively localized public goods where the beneficiaries are not so many that mutual consultation is impossible. A classic case of some villagers trying to reach agreement on draining a common meadow was described by Hume (1740), and more recently analysed intensively by Jean Hampton.[7]

A two-person public good problem might be the repair of a road serving only two houses. Both have a right of way, and both

---

[6] Ideally we should put this equation in terms of utilities.
[7] Hampton (1987). Private public good provision is also closely analysed by Jasay (1989), especially chs 6–8. Both give further references to a large literature.

householders would be willing to pay half the cost of repairs. This might be a prisoners' dilemma in that the best strategem for each could be to do nothing, because the other might repair the road, or, if not, because a muddy track is a better outcome than incurring the full costs of repairing the road alone. This illustrates the absurdity of regarding such a situation as a non-cooperative one-shot prisoners' dilemma. The two householders would surely get together and bargain about how much each should contribute. There need be no problem of distrust for an escheat account could be used. We would then have the cooperative bargain game where commitments can be made. We are not in the business of exploring such games which would take us too far afield, and is beyond my competence.

The non-cooperative game does not have to be a prisoners' dilemma. It could be the game of 'chicken' as illustrated in Fig. 9.5. Here there is no dominant strategem. Rowena prefers to defect if Colin cooperates, but prefers to cooperate if Colin defects; and similarly for Colin. This would arise if each would repair the road alone, rather than endure the muddy track. Some other consideration would need to be introduced to determine the outcome. It is possible that either Rowena or Colin would repair the road: but they might meet and bargain.

I once found myself in the road repair game. There were seven houses with rights of way. There were no social or business relations between the houses. When I joined, the road was in a very poor state. I obtained an estimate, and devised a schedule of fair shares for each house (since the distances from the main road differed) and wrote to each householder accordingly. There was, I think, no doubt that the benefit exceeded the cost for each householder. All agreed bar one, who still refused after knowing that all the others had accepted; and remained a free-rider throughout.

| | Colin | |
	Cooperate	Defect
Rowena Cooperate	3, 3	1, 4
Rowena Defect	4, 1	0, 0

Figure 9.5. *Utils.*

The others agreed to raise their subscriptions by the required amount of about 17 per cent and the repairs were made (this shows that it was not an assurance game).

What calculation does the householder make, if fully rational by game theory standards? The outcome is uncertain. The rational householder compares the expected benefit of the outcome of not subscribing with that of subscribing. The former is the benefit from the repair multiplied by the probability of it occurring without his or her subscription. The latter is the benefit minus the subscription cost multiplied by the probability of the repair being made when he or she does subscribe. The relative probability is the probability that one's subscription makes all the difference to whether or not the repairs are made. The reader can experiment with figures. My estimate in the actual case is that trying to free-ride would certainly have seemed to be the optimum strategy. If I am right, there was a prisoners' dilemma situation, which could not plausibly be modelled as an indefinitely repeated game. But only one person played the game properly! I did not question the householders' motives. But I have little doubt that moral considerations of some kind played a part. I believe that similar circumstances and outcomes are common. If I am right, this is good news for those who claim that many public goods are provided without recourse to external intervention, but bad news for those who claim that morality arises from agreement.

I would like to draw one further lesson from my road repair. The possibility of making the road public was investigated. But the local council would take over only if the road was first brought up to a standard much higher than that thought adequate by the householders, and at a correspondingly much higher cost. The usual argument has been that without external intervention too little or nothing of a public good would be provided. But it is also possible that government intervention would result in over-provision. Circumstances of public good supply vary widely. The only reasonable conclusion is that the probable costs and benefits need to be realistically assessed case by case.

PUBLIC GOODS AND THE STATE

We have seen that states typically provide a large range of goods, many of which are far from having the defining characteristics of pure public goods. These characteristics imply that such goods cannot be sold piecemeal to individuals. But this does not imply that efficient private provision of essentially public goods is always impossible. However, the general provision of protective services for all members of a large society is surely impossible to arrange without there being some institution which amounts to a state.[8] The services of the institutions of law and order—the courts, the police, and prisons—are not quite pure public goods since their services are sold to a limited extent: but they are nearly so. And national defence is a pure public good, with which one must include foreign policy. Numbers are very important. A few people can often reach a cooperative arrangement to produce something. But when the number is large, the problem of free-riders cannot be overcome without an authority with powers of compulsion.

There are other candidates. Although in theory money could be competitively supplied by private financial institutions, I think that almost all economists would include the provision of a stable currency as a public good which should ultimately be the responsibility of the state. Other economic services are more debatable candidates. Further reference to some of these will be made in Chapter 11.

Some may argue that macroeconomic objectives such as stability, growth, and full employment, should be included as public goods on the grounds that almost everyone benefits from them. I think this would be stretching language too far. Some, for example those who favour much government, may want to make the concept of public goods as inclusive as possible, because it is widely accepted that a proper function of government is the provision of public goods. I am opposed to pre-judging issues by such verbal manipulation. But I am not arguing that the sole function of government is the provision of public goods.

It certainly cannot be argued that redistribution is in general a public good on the ground that everyone benefits from it. Poverty relief is a better candidate. It has been argued that everyone would like to see less poverty, and would therefore gain from its reduction, perhaps by more than the cost. Poverty relief may then be regarded as a proper function of government.

[8] Robert Nozick in *Anarchy, State and Utopia* described how a dominant protective agency could develop from initially competing private protection agencies (probably as a result of economies of scale). It would then be a mini-state.

10

Positive Political Economy

We have in the previous chapters often referred to the government making decisions on behalf of the state. To say that the government decides is to say that a collective decision is made. But we have not discussed how collective decisions are in practice made. We need to ask three questions. First, how is the government constituted? Second, how does it (or any ruling authority) reach decisions? Third, by what principles or aims, if any, is it guided? These are all deep political questions, in which we are interested because of the relationships between the constitution, procedures, and aims of government, and the working of the economy. This is the essential interface of politics and economics and constitutes the subject of positive political economy.

ENDOGENIZING GOVERNMENT

For too long, economists thought of government (and the state) as a benevolent guardian, whose sole purpose was to maximize the welfare of the people, somehow defined (perhaps by the observer or advisor economist!). But in the last quarter of a century this naive simplification has been largely abandoned, and government is now thought of as a positive actor on the economic stage, with its own interests and aims.

This change began in the late 1950s with Downs's *An Economic Theory of Democracy* (1957). But it was the foundation by J.M. Buchanan of the Virginia school of public choice, and Buchanan and Tullock's *The Calculus of Consent* (1962), which inspired much of the later development of the so-called new political economy. This essentially seeks to explain economic policies and trends, by an analysis of what determines the governmental choices that determine them. Some authors seem to regard it as an essential axiom of public choice theory that government maximizes its own utility, where utility is strictly self-interested and does not include the welfare of the citizens: or, where government is not monolithic, every member and every bureaucrat maximizes his personal utility. It is to be expected that politicians and bureaucrats are, in this respect, no different from anyone else. If this is taken to be a defining characteristic of public choice theory then it needs to be distinguished from the 'new political economy'. The latter insists only that government is a positive actor, and cannot be considered to be a mere machine for making collective choices.[1] It tells the economic analyst or advisor that he would be wise to study the aims and power of members of the government.

In our discussion of individual utility in Chapter 1 we defined a utility function as a consistent ordering of choices. There was no need to analyse the motives that lay behind the choices. This was because consistency was of little or no value for predicting behaviour. Furthermore, the positive economist is interested in aggregate behaviour, for instance how much a rise in the price of cigarettes reduces smoking, and not whether a particular person gives it up. But when we come to the behaviour of one or a few politicians we need to change this perspective. The political economist tries to predict or explain the behaviour of a single person, or a handful of people, in circumstances that may not have arisen before. In so doing he may be right to assume that the politician's sole interest is enriching himself: but it is also possible that the politician is concerned, even primarily concerned, with the welfare of the people. Both sorts exist. In what proportions they exist in different countries is, no doubt, very controversial.

Before proceeding further we must distinguish between different kinds of government whose choices are to be considered and if possible explained.

---

[1] Some theorists have envisaged policies emerging from the competition of particular interests in the 'political market place', with the government acting merely as an auctioneer or clearing house. This seems even more fanciful than the benevolent guardian theory of government. On all this see Bhagwati (1990).

DEMOCRATIC AND AUTHORITARIAN GOVERNMENT

We define a democratic government as one that can be peacefully constituted and dismissed by vote of the people in accordance with recognized procedures. Who are the people? In other words, who is entitled to vote? Athens was the original democracy, but slaves were excluded. Switzerland has long been thought of as a democracy, although women had no vote until very recently. For analytic purposes all that matters is that there is a large number of voters, too large to constitute a clique, or to act as the central committee of a political party.

At the opposite extreme is pure dictatorship. The dictator effectively controls all the instruments of power. He must make sure that the army and the police are loyal, but is otherwise beholden to no one. His aims may range (and have ranged) from enriching himself and his family, to the achievement of some ideologically determined enterprise, such as genocide; they could even include the welfare of the people (as defined by himself), although this is likely to be an instrument for some other end.

There are lesser degrees of dictatorship. The chairman of the central committee of a single political party may or may not be constrained by the need for some consensus among its elite. But when there are no elections, or only rigged elections, such governments are essentially autocratic, and come close to pure dictatorship. They may also be described as autonomous, that is they are free to pursue their own ends. We are not concerned with how such autocratic governments were originally constituted.

An essential difference is that a democratically constituted government depends for its continued existence on votes. An elected government's power is constrained by the need for re-election, that is by the need to please the voters. But it may also be constrained by the institutions of the state. It may be bound by a constitution. The constitution may be constitutionally changed; but if it is flouted the government is unlikely to remain democratic by our definition. For instance, Mrs Gandhi's declaration of an Emergency in India in 1975 flouted the spirit of the constitution even if it was technically legal. The government during the Emergency ceased to be democratic, for it could be displaced only with her agreement, or by force.

The bureaucracy may also constrain the government. Students of politics have distinguished a hybrid state they call 'bureaucratic authoritarian'. Governments, whether relatively dictatorial or democratic, may come and go, but the bureaucracy goes on forever; and may acquire such power that it can shackle government and pursue its own objectives, its own wealth and power and their continuance.

These complications do not alter the fact that voting is an essential procedure in a democratic state. Government is constituted by voting. Voting is also, of course, a customary method of arriving at collective choices in many subsidiary institutions, and this may to some extent be true when the national government is itself dictatorial. We need to turn to an analysis of voting and collective choice, before returning to a discussion of how economic policies are actually made.

COLLECTIVE CHOICE AND VOTING

When people would choose differently between alternatives, how are their preferences somehow amalgamated so that a collective choice is made? Voting is the normal method. It may not be a very good method. Consider three selectors—A, B, and C; and two candidates—X and Y. A is wise, well-informed, and passionately wants X. B and C, who both have a mild, ill-considered preference for Y, together outvote A.

Voting is a still more dubious method when there are three candidates—X, Y, and Z. We may then have the famous voting paradox discovered by Condorcet in 1785 and elaborated by Duncan Black (1948). A prefers X to Y, and Y to Z; B prefers Z to X, and X to Y; C prefers Y to Z, and Z to X. In pairwise voting, provided voters vote in accordance with their preferences, X gets a majority over Y, Y over Z, and Z over X. If all pairs are considered one just goes round in a circle, and no candidate is chosen. If a majority is interpreted as a collective or social preference, and transitivity of preference is taken as axiomatic, then we have a contradiction.

If a losing candidate is eliminated from further voting in order to secure an election, then the election depends on the order of voting. If X and Y are first voted on, then Y is eliminated and Z elected. If Y and Z are first voted on, then Z is eliminated and X elected. If Z and

X are first voted on, X is eliminated and Y elected. Obviously, he who controls the order of voting can get who he wants.

The voting paradox was generalized by K.J. Arrow (1951). Assume that there are at least two choosers and three possibilities. Each chooser is assumed to have a consistent (transitive, reflexive) ordering of the possibilities. The orderings are unrestricted. The question is whether a consistent collective order can be constructed which does not break certain obvious rules of correspondence with the individual orders, such as that if X ranks higher than Y in every chooser's order, then it must not rank lower in the social order. The answer is that no consistent social order is possible which does not coincide with that of some chooser. Such an order is deemed to be dictatorial. This is commonly expressed by the proposition that no non-dictatorial Social Welfare Function is possible.[2]

Arrow's theorem attracted great interest, and spawned a large literature of attempts to circumvent it.[3] This was partly because it seemed to have the important ideological implication that Rousseau's General Will was nonsensical. However, others (myself anyway!) did not think that they needed Arrow's demonstration to convince them of this.[4]

The practical importance of the voting paradox and Arrow's theorem is also very slight. This is for various reasons. Often there are only two choices. When there are more possibilities, pairwise voting is rare (though this could be to some extent because procedures are determined by sophisticated persons who are aware of the voting paradox). United Kingdom electors are not asked to rank Conservative, Liberal, and Labour. Even if they were, most preferences would be single-peaked which would rule out a contradiction.[5] Finally, electors may indulge in strategic voting or in

[2] I have not presented the argument rigorously. For a more rigorous account that is also more accessible than that of Arrow himself, see William Vickrey, 'Utility, Strategy, and Social Decision Rules', *Q.J.E.* Vol. 74 (1960), reprinted in Barry and Hardin (eds) (1982). This volume also contains a reprint of my critique of Arrow's theory, 'Social Choice and Individual Values' (1952). The proof of Arrow's theorem relies on the 'independence of irrelevant alternatives', an axiom which rules out ranking procedures other than the pairwise comparisons of the possibilities that produce the paradox of voting. See Gordon Tullock, 'Appendix 2' in Buchanan and Tullock (1962).

[3] It has also spawned three Nobel prizes. Seldom have so many clever people spent so much time on a matter of so little importance.

[4] See Little (1952).

[5] If possibilities can be arranged in a line in such a way that a chooser would always choose a possibility closer to his first choice than one further away, then his

log rolling,[6] which may also rule out any voting paradox. Voting has a large literature, and we cannot go into all its subtleties.[7] In particular, we neglect the important subject of proportional representation. We shall select a few features of simple majority voting which seem to be especially relevant when considering its desirability as a method of arriving at public collective decisions.

Suppose there is some public project which will be financed by taxation that bears equally on all, but does not benefit everyone equally. Such a project may get a majority vote even although its total cost exceeds its total benefit. This is quite general, but can be simply illustrated in a three-person case. The cost is 99, and A, B, and C would each get an addition to their tax bills of 33. A and B each get a benefit of 40, and so vote for the project. C gets nothing. The total benefit is only 80 and the cost is 99. A and B each get a net gain of 7, and C loses 33. It may immediately be objected that money may not be worth the same to A, B, and C. It might be that a redistribution from C to A and B was desirable. But there is a better way of bringing it about. C gives, say, 10 to A and B; and they are then all better-off than with the project.

J. de V. Graaff (1962) has analysed the role of popularity. He argued that whether a project, or change of policy, is popular is a relevant bit of information. But popularity is never a sufficient reason to recommend a project, nor unpopularity a sufficient reason to advise against. In particular, as in the above case, a project or policy may be popular only on distributional grounds; in which case redistribution without the project should be considered. I believe that carrying out generally harmful but popular projects is a serious and common disadvantage of democratic decision-making.

Voting is a bad way of distributing anything. Suppose there is a pile of manna. If there are two claimants, the only majority is when both agree, but this is ruled out by the assumption of self-interested

choices are single-peaked. Thus if we arrange possibilities in the order X Y Z, then the chooser with single-peaked preferences who puts X first must not choose Z before Y. Thus X Z Y, and similarly Z X Y, are ruled out. This removes the voting paradox as Duncan Black discovered.

[6] Log rolling is persuading someone to change his vote in return for a similar favour.

[7] The reader may consult Dennis C. Mueller, *Public Choice II*, 1989, which also contains many further references.

rationality. Suppose, then, that there are three claimants—A, B, and C. Any two, say A and B, can vote to get half each and leave C with nothing. But then C will approach A (or B) and propose, say, a division of 51/100 for A and 49/100 for C, leaving B with nothing. A accepts. But B can then approach C and suggest a half for himself and C, leaving nothing for A. There is no solution. Income or wealth cannot generally be assigned by democratic vote. This has far-reaching consequences, that have been convincingly explored by Dan Usher (1981) in a neglected book. We refer to this again in Chapter 11.

It has often been pointed out that a majority can tyranically exploit a minority, but in the above case there can be no permanent majority. Every coalition can be overthrown by another. Voting paradoxes have indeed been praised as a safeguard against the tyranny of the majority. 'The fact that [majority] decisions may be formally inconsistent provides one of the most important safe-guards against abuse through this form of the voting system.'[8]

Nevertheless, there can be minorities that, for social or ethnic reasons, are unable to form effective voting coalitions. An elected majority government could exploit them, say by specially targeted taxation. This could be a case where an elected majority in effect assigned income. It seems that democratic assignment of income or wealth is either impossible or undesirable. Minorities may be insufficiently protected by voting paradoxes. They then have to rely on acceptance of the view that there are things which no person or government may do to people; or to socially, culturally, or ethnically defined groups of people. This would include targeted taxation or other restrictions on freedom. This does not rule out taxing rich people more than poor people, for rich and poor do not constitute groups or communities. But governments also take decisions that directly influence the income of definable groups with particular interests such as farmers, trade unionists, small business men, and others. We return to the consequences of such partial assignments in Chapter 11.

Direct voting on national government projects or policies, which affect the distribution of wealth, does not normally take place in a democracy. Voters choose parties, which either singly or in coalition form governments. There may be two parties, one of which

[8] J.M. Buchanan (1954).

appeals most to the rich and the other to the poor. There are also floating voters in the middle. This may seem rather like three persons trying to divide a heap of manna. Fortunately, wealth is not easily and quickly redistributed like manna, and there are issues other than distribution. So we do not have a situation where after every election the rich become the poor, and the poor become the rich, as floating voters switch. However, there is a widely believed theory that parties concentrate their favours on the median voter.[9]

The median voter is the one with the same number of persons richer than he, as there are poorer. Suppose there are 101 voters and two parties. The poorer 50 persons can be relied on to vote for the supposedly pro-poor party, and the richer 50 for the supposedly pro-rich party. Both parties are then only concerned to win over the median voter (if the number of voters is even, say 100, then, numbering from the poorest, the pro-poor party has to win over the 51st voter and the pro-rich party the 50th). Whether there is any statistical evidence that income distribution has shifted over time in favour of people with middle incomes I do not know. Attempts to test the theory are discussed in Mueller (1989). Where there are many parties and many issues, the median voter theory loses its simple appeal. And in some countries there are indeed many parties appealing especially to particular regional, ethnic, social, linguistic, or religious groupings. India is the extreme example of a democracy of which this is true.

Before leaving the subject of voting we must take note of another important paradox. If people were rational and self-interested, they would never vote in national elections, or in any election when the number of potential voters was very large. The chance of any one vote making a difference to the outcome is so small that it is certainly not worth the effort needed to go to the polling station or postbox. It may be objected that if everyone thus calculated the net expected benefit, then no one would vote, in which case everyone's vote would be decisive—another paradox! But with many repeated national elections one could reach an equilibrium with an extremely low expected turnout, low enough for it to be just worth voting. Turnouts are far higher than this, and so one has to conclude that

[9] The economist Harold Hotelling first proposed the theorem in 'Stability in Competition'. *Economic Journal*, 39, March 1929.

voters vote for reasons other than enlightened self-interest.[10] They may, for instance, believe that it is a civic duty to vote. Finally, it should be noted that it is not rational for an individual voter to give even a moment's thought to which outcome would be in his best interest. Yet much theorizing, such as the median voter theorem, depends upon voters' well-informed, self-interested rationality. The theory of the very ill-informed voter suggests that he may be influenced by the crudest propaganda.

ECONOMIC POLICY UNDER RELATIVELY AUTONOMOUS GOVERNMENT

Public choice explanations will vary according to the autonomy of the government; the more autonomous the greater the importance of the aims of the chief executive himself and his essential support- ers—his entourage, the bureaucratic elite, and the military. Revenue is likely to be a prime consideration as it is needed for the enrichment of the dictator and his cronies. Large capital-intensive projects will be favoured for the kickbacks available. The military will also be interested in steel and other industrial projects that lead to some national capacity to produce armaments. Furthermore, the more autonomy the more room there is for dogma to play a part. The wel- fare of the mass of the people is not likely to be a major consideration, even regarded as an instrument for remaining in power.

The above a priori expectations have, in recent years, been real- ized especially but not exclusively in developing countries. There have been a good many dictators who have enriched themselves by hundreds of millions, even billions, of dollars; and some of them have at the same time adopted policies which led to stagnation or a serious fall in the standard of living of the mass of the people. But this is not true of all dictatorships. South Korea, Taiwan, and Singapore, were effectively dictatorships in their periods of unprecedented growth (and poverty relief). The fourth member of the so-called 'gang of four', Hong Kong, was a crown colony with an autocratic government. And General Pinochet, whatever the evils of his repression of opposition, fathered policies which set Chile on the road to economic success and poverty relief. A dictator

---

[10] There have been many attempts to explain voting turnout in national elections. None is convincing; see Green and Shapiro (1994), ch. 4.

may understand that a thriving economy that produces a rising standard of living for most people is also most conducive to sustained enrichment of himself and his close supporters. But he may not! The upshot seems to be that no reliable general truths apply to essentially autocratic governments. The importance of individuals, with their varying desires and beliefs, is too great. It is for this reason that much of political economy is concerned only with democracies. However, developing countries, which are nearly all autocracies, are further considered below.

ECONOMIC POLICY UNDER DEMOCRACY

We turn to less autonomous governments which have to win votes. Among them there is another important distinction, between those with a relatively homogeneous electorate, and those where there is a manifold of particular interests, based on tribe, race, language, religion, and inherited culture. Such electorates may be termed 'factional'. In the former, differences of political relevance between persons are mainly those of wealth and economic status: whether one is an employer, employee, or self-employed; whether one is a member of a recognized profession or a casual worker, and so forth. In such an economy there is likely to be only two or three major political parties, whose supporters differ mainly in wealth, and economic or social status. In the latter, the government will often be a coalition of several, even many, parties representing different factions. Thus economic circumstances—the relations of production as Marxists would say—are most likely to be major determinants of economic policies when the electorate is relatively homogeneous. When it is heterogeneous, factional interests tend to cut across narrower economic interests. Most of the older industrialized countries of North America and Western Europe, but also Japan, are relatively homogeneous. They are also democracies, and have been so for many years. It is no accident that public choice theory and the new political economy have been applied mostly to industrialized countries. Most developing countries are more heterogeneous than the industrialized countries, and most of them have been near dictatorships for most of the past 50 years. The political economy of these countries is therefore of a rather different hue to that of the industrialized countries, and we have a separate section on them below.

MODELLING POLITICAL ECONOMY
EXPLANATIONS OF POLICIES AND TRENDS

The main aim of democratic governments is to remain in power. They respond to unorganized voters in general, but also to organized groups with special interests; these latter also influence voters. However, there may be 'voting room' for a government to try to achieve its own aims which may not be popular, or to satisfy special interest groups who lobby them in various ways, whether legally or corruptly. To complicate matters further, the government is not normally monolithic. It consists of various ministries and agencies, which probably have their own distinct agenda. The institutional procedures by which issues are addressed and decisions reached also vary from government to government. Individual citizens may express their preferences economically by voting for one party or another, or less economically by subscribing to a party's or a candidate's funds, or by joining some influential grouping.

From the above description it is clear that political decisions and outcomes can be modelled in many ways, and that varying assumptions about individual and institutional behaviour affect the working of the different models. Many such models are discussed in recent surveys and textbooks. Many incorporate the median voter theorem, but otherwise there is little uniformity. One is tempted to suggest that substituting the median voter for the average voter is the main theoretical contribution of public choice theory. More important has been the impetus to bring expected governmental behaviour into any analysis of the formation of economic policy. The various models and applications have been too numerous for a survey in this introductory book. Reference may be made to D.C. Mueller (1989), Torsten Persson and Guido Tabellini (2000), and Allan Drazen (2000). I select only two issues that have been much studied in the context of the democratic industrialized countries; protection, and the growth of government.[11]

---

[11] But more success has, perhaps, been achieved in measuring the effects of political insitutions. For instance, whether or not US State Governors are re-electable seems to have some influence on state tax and expenditure decisions (Timothy Besley and Anne Case, 1995); and the presence of formal fiscal requirements speeds up fiscal adjustment (James M. Poterba, 1994). The large number of States of the USA is very helpful for investigating political economy, and other sociological or purely political relationships.

THE POLITICAL ECONOMY OF PROTECTION IN INDUSTRIALIZED COUNTRIES

A standard explanation of protection is that it shifts the distribution of income towards those with political influence. The theory derives from the Stolper-Samuelson theorem[12] and the median voter theorem. A country such as the USA with a relatively high capital/labour ratio, will have relatively high wages, and import relatively labour-intensive goods which moderate the demand for labour. Import duties or quotas will therefore benefit labour relative to those who live on capital.[13] The median voter, whose endowment is more labour intensive than the average, will therefore favour protection. High protection in Argentina and Australia has also been explained as a means of redistributing income from pastoralists to industrial workers.

Certain features of US protection are at least consistent with this theory. Thus protection has declined over time with the relative strength of labour; and labour-intensive industries are most protected. Protection increases when there is a recession or when the terms of trade improve, both of these events hurting labour. However, the theory fails to explain the differing political attitudes of democrats and republicans towards protection, or the fact that republican presidents have, without exception, been more protectionist than democratic presidents.[14]

Anne Krueger's study of protection[15] for the US sugar industry casts doubt on the possibility of any theoretical explanation of protection. The cost to the economy has been huge but very few people have gained anything: indeed, many of those who lobbied for the programme could not reasonably have expected to gain. A main point she makes is that a programme tends with time to become more complex, to collect unexpected adherents, to have unexpected consequences leading to further interventions, and to create vested interests for those who understand its complexity.

---

[12] W.F. Stolper and P.A. Samuelson (1941).

[13] An alternative three-factor model can lead to a tariff raising the returns to both factors in a particular industry. For a survey of various models of the political determination of protection see T.N. Srinivasan (1991).

[14] See Stephen P. Magee, 'The Political Economy of US Protection' in Herbert Giersch (ed.), 1987.   [15] Krueger (1990).

Finally, explaining protection by its distributive effects is not fundamentally satisfactory, not to an economist anyway, because the redistribution could usually, if not always, be more efficiently obtained by subsidy rather than by protection.[16] The question then is 'why do politicians prefer tariffs or non-tariff barriers (NTBs) to more direct support for, say, garment workers'? Perhaps the reason is that subsidies can be attacked on the popular ground that they cost the taxpayers money, while it is hard to organize a lobby against a small rise in the price of shirts. But this is speculation. Further research is needed on conflicts between economic efficiency and politically perceived popularity.

THE GROWTH OF GOVERNMENT IN INDUSTRIALIZED COUNTRIES

The growth of government has alarmed many people. Table 10.1 gives some figures for government final consumption, and social security transfers, as a percentage of GDP, for the US and non-US OECD countries. Government final consumption comes reasonably close to the current provision of public goods. It excludes investment, and all transfers including interest on the public debt. Social security transfers are given separately. The non-US OECD figures are simple country averages: but the increases are general; in every country the rise in public good provision was significant.

Before the Second World War, expenditures on both public goods and social security were much lower. The war caused a revolution in people's ideas about what government could and should do. There is also probably a ratchet effect: it is politically easier to build up a service than to reduce it. But these effects had run their course by 1960: the main new public services in health, education, and housing, were in place. In the non-US OECD countries, the provision of public goods rose from 12.3 per cent of GDP to 15.9 per cent in the 35 years from 1960 to 1995, despite a significant fall in defence expenditure. In the USA, public good provision fell a little, but it would have risen significantly if it had not been for a large fall in defence expenditure. The rise was continuous except for the period 1985–89 when the UK and many other

---

[16] This is emphasized by Dani Rodrick (1995).

Table 10.1. *Government Expenditure in OECD Countries—% of GDP*

		1960	1974	1985	1989	1995
Government Final	Non-USA	12.3	14.8	16.2	15.4	15.9
Consumption	USA	16.6	17.6	17.8	17.2	15.8
Social Security	Non-USA	8.5	11.3	15.3	14.8	17.6
Transfers	USA	5.1	9.6	10.8	10.6	13.1

countries took active steps to reduce expenditure. But from 1989 to 1995 the percentage rose again for most of the OECD, while the USA continued to reduce the percentage to below what it had been in 1960, largely because of a fall in defence expenditure.

Are there demand-side reasons for the rise in expenditure on non-defence public goods and services in the non-US OECD countries? Estimates of the income elasticity of demand for public goods and services suggest that it does not differ significantly from one. So with no change in prices, demand would have risen in the same proportion as national income. But productivity in the public sector has risen by less than in the private sector, so there must have been a relative rise in the cost of public goods and services. Since the price elasticity of demand is less than one, this implies an increase in demand. This is known as the 'Baumol effect'. D.C. Mueller on whom I rely for the statements in this paragraph, suggests that this effect accounts for about one-quarter of the growth of public good expenditure in the OECD countries.[17] This leaves a lot to be explained. Tentative suggestions include ageing of the population and some breakup of family life, both of which increase dependence on public goods provided by the state.

The Baumol effect is essentially saying that if the government had continued to do no more than supply the demand for those public goods which it supplied in 1960, expenditure would have risen only by about a quarter of the actual rise. The rest may have been partly in response to perceived public opinion, partly due to self-serving bureaucratic initiatives, or to yielding to powerful lobbying by special interests. Even if the main cause has been responsiveness to public opinion—the desire of government to win

[17] D.C. Mueller (1989), pp. 322–6.

votes—that does not show that the increase was desirable for the long-run welfare of the people (or, synonomously, the wealth of the nation). Even if people were very well-informed about costs, popularity would not, as we have seen, be sufficient for a project or policy to be desirable for the wealth of the nation.

We have considered the demand for public goods and services. But they must be paid for by taxation, and so the willingness to be taxed must also be taken into account. Democratic governments are as concerned with losing votes by raising taxes as they are with winning them by good public services. They may also be concerned that high taxation is a disincentive to work and take risks, and may thus reduce both production and growth. The strength of these relationships is much debated and extremely difficult to assess. We lack the space and expertise that would be needed for a well-considered view.

Taxation is also, of course, required for the other main item of public expenditure—social security transfers. They include public pensions, family allowances, old-age benefits, disability benefit, and unemployment relief. As Table 10.1 shows, they have grown a good deal faster than public goods. In the the non-US OECD the proportion of GDP spent doubled from 8.5 per cent to 17.6 per cent between 1960 and 1995. The chief albeit weak theoretical explanation of personal transfers is the median voter theorem. Suppose that there are n voters, and that national income is £$100n$. The mean income is £100. A per caput subsidy of £1 is given and financed by a proportional one per cent income tax. If one's income is less than the mean, one gets £1 as subsidy and pays less than £1 in tax. So if the median income is less than the mean, the median voter gains. Hence the combination of a rise in taxation and subsidies wins votes. This may explain transfers but not changes in transfers. Starting with an equilibrium distribution in which the net median income equals the mean, an increase in the income of the rich will drive the median below the mean, and increase the popularity of transfers: but a fall in the income of the poor would have the opposite effect, tending to reduce transfers. So changes in equality can go either way, and I do not know of any convincing work relating the value of transfers to inequality. It should be noted that, although we have treated redistributive transfers and public good provision separately, the public provision of health and education also has redistributive effects, and is intended to have them. Finally, we should note that not all transfers go to the poor; for instance, wealthy old people receive state pensions and many other concessions.

It seems that we know very little about the forces that drive the increase in government expenditure as a proportion of national income, and that the public choice literature has not added much.

PROTECTION AND IMPORT SUBSTITUTION IN DEVELOPING COUNTRIES

The major phenomenon to be explained is protection, and efforts to dismantle it. Protection in developing countries has had a very different rationale to that in the industrialized countries. In the latter, the main reason for protection was redistribution in favour of workers in labour-intensive industries. In most developing countries labour-intensive industry has been handicapped as a result of protection. Only in a very few land-intensive developing countries was redistribution in favour of industrial workers, in relatively capital-intensive industries, a driving reason. Argentina is the main example and compares in this respect with Australia. Explanation must also take notice of the fact that industrialized countries were democracies in the relevant period, while developing countries were almost all autocracies.

In the post-war period, industrialization by means of import substitution behind high tariffs or import quotas, or both, became an almost universal policy in the developing world as soon as countries not already independent became so. To some extent import substitution had started as a policy in Latin America between the wars, but it was not the dogma that it subsequently became. What led to this near universal policy was an urge to develop fast, combined with distrust of the price mechanism in general, and free trade in particular. The latter was believed by many in developing countries to have been the instrument by which the industrialized countries of the centre exploited the periphery. Distrust of the price mechanism was encouraged by almost all the most influential economist members of the development establishment of the 1950s and early 1960s. Excessive government expenditure led to inflation and a current account deficit on the balance of payments. It was thought that devaluation would worsen the terms of trade (exports of manufactures were not envisaged), and therefore import controls were instituted. Trade was repressed by the controls and overvaluation of the currency; and there was also financial repression (low stocks of money relative to national income) as a result of inflation and interest rate controls. The resulting shortages led to a relatively capital-intensive industrial development. Import substitution seemed natural, and became a dogma. This story is an old hat and has been repeated in countless publications.

The new political economy has not added anything to the story. The universality of import substitution requires us to look for some common features. These were (a) the drive to develop; (b) the fear of trade; (c) fixed exchange rates under Bretton Woods combined with a fear of devaluation; (d) bad advice from development economists who reinforced the anti-trade prejudice. Differences between economies and differences in the degree of autocracy of government were apparently irrelevant. Nor did it matter whether some charismatic ruler was mainly concerned to further his own fortune, to secure the independence of the country, or to maximize the welfare of the people. The policy of import substitution was seen as an essential instrument for all such ends. It was a powerful intellectual fashion that silenced analysis and criticism in most countries for about 20 years.[18]

It is interesting that K.Y. Yin, then Economics Minister of Taiwan, recognized the disadvantages of import substitution in the 1950s.[19] Taiwan changed course in the 1960s, soon followed by Korea and Singapore. All had strong and determined leaders, who became convinced that more open policies should be pursued. Men and ideas matter a lot. However, this does not imply that autocratic government is necessary for reform.

POLICY REFORM IN DEVELOPING COUNTRIES

In the 1970s and early 1980s many developing countries tried to adopt more open less repressive regimes, usually in a half-hearted way with limited success. These attempts have been described by many authors without taking a specifically political economy point

---

[18] D. Lal has an interesting and more complex analysis of protection in developing countries, distinguishing labour- and land-abundant countries under 'factional' states where rival groups with different factor endowments determine policy. See D. Lal and H. Myint (1996), esp. ch. 6. [19] K.Y. Yin (1954).

of view.[20] But it was only after the 1982 debt crisis that many countries, often under the guidance and with the conditional financial support of the IMF and IBRD, attempted thorough structural reforms featuring far greater openness to trade and capital movements.

What are structural reforms? Are they good? There is by now a broad consensus among economists on what constitutes the main elements of good economic policy. A government should handle its expenditure and taxes, and its foreign borrowing, in a manner that is sustainable in the long run. It should avoid inflation of more than a few percentage points per annum. It should prefer reliance on the price mechanism to regulation in most areas of the economy. It should permit free trade with other countries subject only to moderate tariffs. It should permit the free movement of capital (there is perhaps less than consensus on this point). The structural reforms we are considering are those that lead to good economic policy as thus defined, where previously one or more of the elements of good policy was clearly absent. Achievement of the broad reforms as described usually requires many detailed reforms in particular markets or sectors of the economy, which may be politically difficult.

In John Williamson (ed.), 1994, structural reforms in 17 countries were examined with the intention of discovering the political economy conditions most probably required for the success of the reforms. By success is meant that there is little likelihood of retreat; in other words, the reforms seem to be consolidated. The countries were chosen for success: only in two cases, Brazil and Peru, was it doubtful. The countries included were from what would previously have been called the first, second, and third worlds. The third-world countries, that is developing countries, included were Brazil, Chile, Columbia, Indonesia, Korea, Mexico, Peru, and Turkey. The absence of any African country is notable: it was thought that none had achieved a consolidated reform. Bates and Krueger (1993) report on similar research for eight developing countries: Egypt and Ghana were included, and so was Zambia, a clear case of failure. In addition to these, there are also important works by political scientists on the political economy of reform.[21]

---

[20] Among others see Krueger (1978), Bhagwati (1979), Williamson (1990), Michaely *et al.* (1991).
[21] For instance, Haggard and Kaufman (eds), 1992, and Nelson (ed.), 1990.

We can give only a résumé of the more salient and surprising results, that are very widely agreed by the many authors of the underlying studies. Where very relevant I refer also to India; although not included in the above studies, I have some acquaintance with its reforms.[22]

We begin with the political background. There was no relationship between economic reform and authoritarianism. This was despite the common-sense view that it should be easier for a dictator than a democratic government to implement changes which inevitably harm some interests; and despite the fact that some of the reforms, for example, in Chile, Korea, and Turkey, were achieved only after military intervention. However, all the authoritarian governments showed much concern either with the public at large or with special interests, while political institutions allowed democracies considerable room for manoeuvre without alienating the electorate. None of the governments could be considered 'unitary', that is, possessing a single utility function. Whether authoritarian or democratic, all the developing country governments were centre or right wing, along the conventional political spectrum. A more leftist tendency was found only in the more industrialized countries.

Most of the reform movements began with a crisis, usually one of very high inflation, or a large balance of payments deficit combined with a drying up of credit so that essential imports could not be bought. Since reform is never politically easy, it is not surprising that it usually starts from a situation where something has to be done. But stabilization, involving fiscal cutbacks, and import controls or devaluation, has often occurred without any thoroughgoing structural reform. More than crisis was required. Import substitution had run out of steam as a locomotive. Independently, ideology was also changing, as more leaders and economic advisors had been educated in North American universities, and the influence of the old development establishment, with its continental European roots, waned. The failure of the USSR model helped, and gradually the extraordinary success of the 'gang of four' entered the mind-set of policy makers. World Bank and IMF persuasion, and loan conditionality were also important. It is interesting that the impulse to reform always came from within the government itself, even if prodded by the international institutions, and not from special interests such as the business community.

Many reform initiatives have failed over the years. What makes for success? There are no conditions that can be described as necessary or sufficient. But some accompany success more often than not. The following suggest themselves:

- a central executive with strong budgetary control
- a determined charismatic leader with a good political base
- external aid (in the case of poor countries)
- a team of economists with strong political backing to design and explain the reforms
- some media support

The first two conditions are amply exemplified and need no comment. Every structural reform, especially when it has to be combined with stabilization, initially harms some interests. The harm is likely to be concentrated, and the benefits longer-term and diffuse. Many who would ultimately benefit may not realize this, or think it not worth the risk. Compensation of the immediate probable losers is therefore called for, and this is why external aid can be essential.

The mention of a team of economists needs further comment, although the 'Chicago boys' in Chile, and the 'Berkeley mafia' in Indonesia have become famous in development circles. In Indonesia there were unfortunately two teams of technocrats, the economists and the engineers. The economy did well when the economists had the president's ear, and became troubled when the engineers were favoured. The same was true of Korea after 1973. More generally, the 1980s and 1990s have been years of increasing reform backed by economists. In Mexico, presidents Salinas and Zedillo were economists. In India, an economist, the finance minister Manmohan Singh, backed by a strong team in the ministry, at last in 1991 initiated important reforms: unfortunately they slowed to a trickle and are still not fully secure because the political base in this great federal democracy was lost, and there are still important vested interests to overcome. Among others, Domingo Cavallo, who orchestrated Argentina's reforms in the 1990s, is an economist. In Turkey, the economist Turgut Ozal was a key figure in reform, and very recently the ex-World Bank economist Kemal Dervis has become finance minister.

In what sense is all this research on economic reform an exercise in the new political economy? It is, of course, research which concentrates on the determination of governmental economic decisions. From an economist's point of view, therefore, this is certainly political economy. But what has the discipline of economics contributed? Have political scientists much to learn from their economic collaborators or colleagues?[23] My impression is not much! There is little use of economic tools such as maximizing expected utility, of rational expectations, of trade-offs, or of Nash equilibria. The analogue of a political market place is, as we have already suggested, false.

AN INTERIM JEJUNE REPORT ON ENDOGENIZING GOVERNMENT

The economic analyst may describe what he believes to be optimum policies and procedures for a country. He may ignore the government, hoping that one day his designs will be influential, even if no one is likely to listen now. But if he is in no such ivory tower, he must not ignore government. If he does, he may in turn be ignored, or he will find his policies distorted or ineffectively implemented. The same may happen if he does not ignore, but misunderstands the government or, as the economist might say, if he has a wrong model of the government. It follows that the normative economist must study both what the government thinks will follow from the actions it takes, and whether it will approve these supposed outcomes. He can, of course, seek to change the government's idea of the consequences that would follow from some policy, where he believes it wrong.

There is no doubt that the government should in this sense be endogenized. It is a very important actor, whose behaviour is crucial for the success of the play, often named 'Reform'. This cannot be doubted. What can be doubted is whether the introduction of economic concepts into the study of government has added much to the understanding of its behaviour. The economist is at home with the concepts of individuals and firms. They are unitary actors who

[23] See Bates, Haggard, and Nelson, 'A Critique by Political Scientists' in Meier (ed.), 1991. See also Green and Shapiro (1994) for a more general critique of rational choice theory.

can be supposed to have utility or profit functions. The same is not true of states and governments. It is true that some insights may be gained by regarding the state as a unitary actor.[24] But this is seldom true when it comes to particular states at particular times. Nor is the state merely a mediator of particular divergent private interests.

I think that the great difficulty of modelling the state is the principal reason why so few surprising or firm conclusions follow from the already large amount of study of reform in developing countries and of particular policies in industrialized countries. This is not to say that the student will not have learned a good deal about what to look out for in trying to explain and understand governments' behaviour. The search will go on, but success may come slowly.

---

[24] I have in mind Jasay's *The State* (1985) whose dramatic opening sentence is 'What would you do if *you* were the state?'

11

Normative Political Economy

Chapter 10 was mainly concerned with positive political economy, with how economic policies are determined not with how they should be determined. This was an essential part of the interface of politics and economics. But it was only indirectly relevant to one of our chief concerns in this book, that is how much government there should be. We now turn to two issues that are directly relevant to this normative question.

FURTHER CONSIDERATION OF GOVERNMENT AND DISTRIBUTION

It was pointed out in Chapter 10 that the assignment of wealth, that is the determination of how much wealth accrues to different people or groups either cannot be made by voting, or should not be when it might involve the exploitation of minorities. How then should the distribution of wealth be determined in a democracy?

Earlier we accepted that some redistribution of wealth is a justifiable function of government. But it was argued that such redistribution should be on grounds of personal poverty, and not, except perhaps in rare circumstances of bad luck, membership of some group. Good reasons of a humanitarian kind can be forcefully advanced for anonymous redistribution from wealthier persons to the very poor, although who is to count as very poor may be arguable. No such grounds can be advanced for redistributing wealth from one group of persons, whether defined by profession, occupation, location, race, age, or gender, to another. There is no principle of morality or justice governing how much, on average, members of different groups should receive. There is thus no non-economic reason why university lecturers should earn twice as much as dustmen and half as much as civil servants of comparable expertise (or whatever the relatives are). In other words, there is no reason apart from the supply of and demand for their services. If the government decides to shift wealth from one such group to another, or to benefit a group at the expense of taxpayers in general, it may be satisfying its own preferences, or those of some of its members: more likely, it is capitulating to insistent lobbying or threats by a group that can inflict some damage to the economy.

Dan Usher emphasized, in the work we referred to in Chapter 10, that there is no moral principle by which such distributional issues can be decided.[1] Furthermore, if they are decided politically, they cannot be decided democratically. He concluded that if democracy is to survive there must be some apolitical system that, to a large extent, determines distributional outcomes. This system is that of a competitive market. Of course, government is inevitably faced with the need to decide many issues which affect distribution. Often it can and does itself rely on competition, as when public salaries are set in line with similar private employment. But this solution may not always be viable, as when the government is faced with a strong trade union. Since it cannot plead that it does not have the money, it is in a weak position. In many developing countries, in my experience, public sector employees are paid much more than their supply price in the private sector. Government cannot altogether avoid distributional problems and conflict, but they should where possible reduce the extent to which they determine the relative wealth or income of different groups or sectors of society. If distribution is determined to a large extent politically then corruption is encouraged, and much political activity is reduced to an unattractive fight for personal and group advantages. Democracy is at risk.

Since the distribution of income and wealth should be largely determined by markets, it is very important that they are competitive. If they are not, then some groups, and even a few individuals may be able to determine or at least significantly influence their own incomes, which is not politically or morally acceptable. It follows that an important function of democratic government is to enforce competition so far as is possible.

This analysis fits in well with the important work of the late Mancur Olson.[2] He analysed the formation of groups with a special interest in increasing their share of national income. The formation of such groups is not easy, because of the free-rider problem. Thus

---

[1] Usher (1981)   [2] Mancur Olson (1965, 1982).

a worker can enjoy any benefits a trade union might gain without paying dues, hence the demand for 'closed shops'. The larger the group the more difficult it is to form. Olson believed that 'selective incentives' have been successfully used to overcome the free-rider problem. Nevertheless, the formation of 'distributional coalitions', as he termed them, took time. However, their number and strength would gradually increase, especially in industrialized countries, at least in peacetime. The main distributional coalitions are monopolies and cartels, employers' and professional associations, and trade unions. These institutions cause a maldistribution of resources, are slow to adapt and take decisions, and are generally opposed to innovation. Their increasing strength results in national sclerosis and slow growth. Rapid growth may resume after a war or revolution because the old coalitions are broken. Olson claims that his theory is at least consistent with history, citing among other instances Germany, France, and Japan after the Second World War, and also the far eastern 'gang of four', in contrast to the slow growth of the UK. But nothing more than consistency can be convincingly claimed, for there are other explanations of relative economic performance.

Some coalitions have valuable activities apart from increasing their share of national income. For instance, trade unions may protect individuals against arbitary discrimination, and professional associations may have a role in protecting consumers against incompetent practitioners. But it is not easy to keep separate any socially useful function that they may have from their distributional or rent-seeking activities. For example, in making regulations intended to ensure the competence of practitioners a professional body may unduly limit entry into that profession, thus raising earnings.

A democratic government's need to promote competition implies that the activities of all distributional coalitions should be limited or controlled. It has long been accepted that legislation is needed to discourage or prohibit cartelization and other monopolistic practices. The case has generally been made by economists on the ground that ability to influence prices results in sub-optimal production. The present case is less esoteric, that neither companies nor persons should be able to determine their own incomes or wealth. While production monopolies have long been unpopular, widespread recognition of the harm that trade unions can do, in terms of distribution as well as production efficiency and progress, is more recent.

If need be, the non-distributional positive functions, if any, of distributional coalitions, may be taken over by government; and, indeed, the welfare state has largely eroded the original human-itarian purpose of trade unions. Distributional coalitions are to be sharply distinguished from coalitions to produce public goods. The former create a need in a democracy for governmental supres-sion or supervision. The latter, as we have argued in Chapter 9, reduce the need for government intervention.

RENT-SEEKING AND CORRUPTION

Rent-seeking is the expenditure of resources to change economic policy, or twist its application in a manner profitable to the rent-seeker. Although examples were previously noticed, it was first named, highlighted, and analysed by Anne Krueger (1974). The idea was further extended and analysed by Bhagwati (1982). This and other work is surveyed by Srinivasan (1991).

Obtaining an import quota is the objective considered by Krueger. The quota is worth the difference between the border price (cum tar-iff) and the domestic price. The seeker may (improbably) obtain the quota with no expenditure of real resources, but it is worth his while to invest them (his time, effort, travel, and other expenses) up to the point where the expected return on them is equal to that in their best alternative use. So the expenditure may come close to the value of the quota. Exactly how much is spent depends on the extent of competition. But anything spent is a cost to the economy which is additional to the cost of the distortion caused by the quota itself. Although rent-seeking does not necessarily involve corruption, part of the cost to the quota-seeker is likely to be a bribe, which is a trans-fer rather than a real cost. To the extent that the bribe reduces the seeker's real expenditure, that is good!

Rent-seeking is not confined to quotas. Whenever there is some effective restriction or control, a gap is opened up between cost and value. The Indian economic regime until very recently was often described as one of 'Permit-raj'. To start any new venture literally dozens of permits would be required. Every such control was a location of rent-seeking. Some probably had no other function. Rent-seeking is also not confined to quantity controls. When there are many different tariff rates there is much time-wasting rent-seeking to raise the rate on a manufacturer's own product and reduce the rates on his inputs, or to shift items to a different tariff division. The same is true of varying excise tax rates or VAT rates. It is for this reason that I have long advocated a single tariff rate, and as few other indirect tax rates as possible.

We have said that rent-seeking does not necessarily involve corruption, but it usually does. It has sometimes been argued that bribery facilitates transactions, and compensates minor officials for inadequate pay, and is not therefore damaging. Such a view is no longer sustainable, if it ever was. Ministers and senior bureaucrats are involved. Many bad investments have been made because of the kick-backs involved. The loss to the economy may be hundreds of times the amount of the bribe paid.

When I first worked in India in 1958, ministers and senior officials were, I believe, with rare exceptions, honest. I have been told that Nehru once personally tore up a permit for a new industrial venture when he learnt that it had been improperly obtained.[3] The change since then has been sadly overwhelming. Most ministers and other politicians are probably corrupt and they have corrupted the civil service. One of the great strengths of Manmohan Singh (Finance Minister from 1991–96) was that he was totally honest and generally so-regarded. Unfortunately, he lacked any personal political base.

Corruption is a serous problem in most developing countries, and in some its extent and depth have been a major cause of economic and political collapse. The most experienced student of corruption, Susan Rose-Ackerman, is in no doubt about its extent and the damage it does.[4] She stresses that although detection and punishment is needed, as well as a well-paid civil service, a more important means of reducing corruption is a reduction in the opportunities that give rise to it. This implies a reduction in the number of controls, and an increase in their simplicity and transparency.

Rent-seeking is the instrument with which persons, firms, and distributive coalitions seek to alter the allocation of wealth in their

---

[3] By T.T. Krishnamachari, Finance Minister at the time, in a personal interview after his retirement.   [4] Rose-Ackerman (1999).

favour. The greater the extent to which the government determines the allocation of wealth, the greater is the opportunity for, and hence certainly the practice of, rent-seeking. Rent-seeking is not confined to trying to change taxes or economic controls in favour of some business or other. It can pervade the political system, which becomes an arena in which passionate contests for economic advantage are fought. In these circumstances democracy is likely to break down, and often has.

PART IV

ETHICS, ECONOMICS, AND POLITICS

12

The Principles of Public Policy

In the Introduction I described this book as a study of the interfaces of ethics, politics, and economics. I thought of these subjects as rubbing up against each other; hence the choice of the word interface. I could have used the phrase overlapping areas, and they are easier to draw, as in Fig. 12.1.

It seems that the overlapping area of each pair drags one inexorably towards a consideration of the third member of the triad. The trinity, that is the common area of all three, may be described as containing the principles of public policy.

A RÉSUMÉ OF PARTS I, II, AND III

Let us start with Part I, Ethics and Economics. Chapter 3 is entitled 'Welfare Economics'. This title could equally well have been

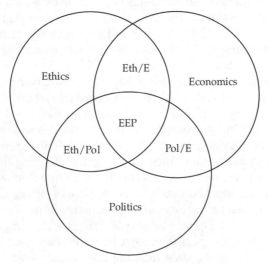

Figure 12.1. *Ethics, Economics, and Politics.*

applied to the whole of Part I. Welfare economics involves comparison of the goodness of different economic states of affairs. The criteria of betterness are derived from economic concepts and analysis. But whether these criteria are acceptable is a moral and political question.

Descriptions of states of affairs generally include the well-being of many people, certainly more than one. So one needs to compare states in which some are better-off and others worse-off, since it is very rare that everyone is better off in one state as compared with another. In order to decide rationally which state is preferred (and chosen if one has the power to choose) it is necessary to compare these differences in welfare and somehow weigh them up together. A distributional judgement must be made which means precisely that one state of affairs is judged to be better (worse) than another although some people are worse-off (better-off). One could leave the discussion at this point—up in the air. But to apply welfare economics to real problems one has to ask who makes the value and distributional judgements required. The answer is 'whoever has to make the decision', that is someone in authority. Welfare economics is in fact applied, in the form of cost-benefit analysis, however rough-and-ready, to public policies and investment projects. So the answer has to be that it is the government, as agent of the state. This is the route by which we reach Part II. We move from the area marked Eth/E to that marked Eth/Pol as in Fig. 12.1. We want to know why the government exists, and what right it has to decide whether one state of affairs is better than another.

Part II is the heart of the book. Chapter 4 considers the role of the state, and the personal freedoms which limit its authority. The idea of a social contract defining and limiting its authority is dismissed. Both state and individual rights arise from the desire of people to live together in a viable society. The state has thus acquired the duty of protecting persons and their property, and ensuring the rule of law. The issue is faced as to whether the state ought to take away property from some to improve the welfare of others. It is concluded that such an infringement of property rights is unjust, but that nevertheless there may be an overriding welfare argument for redistribution. This opens the door to consideration of a more interventionist role for the state than the prevention of wrongdoing, which is the only role of the so-called 'night-watchman' state. For some 200 years utilitarianism has been the main comprehensive doctrine supporting a positive and active role for the state in promoting the welfare of its citizens. Chapter 5 therefore considers utilitarian theory and the question of whose utility the state should try to maximize. This involves discussion of the value of life. The treatment of future people and aliens is also discussed. The chapter constitutes a preliminary defence of utilitarianism, while agreeing that there are some overriding constraints—things which no government or person may do to people whatever the consequences.

Chapter 6 is concerned with attempts, starting in the 1960s, to promote the achievement of equality as a guiding principle for government intervention. The chapter begins by rebutting arguments that utilitarianism is insufficiently egalitarian, but goes on to consider the theories of two of the most prominent anti-utilitarians, John Rawls and Ronald Dworkin. Rawls's highly influential theory is non-teleological: what is good follows from what is right, not vice versa. Rawls is closer to Kant than to Bentham. He believes that valid principles of justice can be derived from the reasoning of self-interested rational persons meeting behind a veil of ignorance which hides from them all knowledge of their tastes and talents, and of what position they would occupy in any society whose basic structure was determined by the principles of justice they are to choose. But we found that the principles that Rawls claims they would choose have no sound basis in reason, and that they bear no relation to one's intuitive ideas of justice. Moreover, we found no reason to suppose that people would feel bound by such principles when the veil was lifted.

This led on to a discussion of the meaning of justice. Justice is about protecting persons and property, enforcing contracts, and supporting important social conventions. This is its primary meaning which does not include what is known as distributive justice. Those in authority, both persons and government, have duties towards those over whom they have authority. The exercise of these duties often involves some distribution of benefits or burdens. There is then a distributor and something to distribute: and this is a requirement of the concept of distributive justice. What is just then depends very much on the circumstances, on what is to be distributed and whether it is divisible. There are no general rules; but customs, conventions, and established expectations may give guidance. Tossing a coin is often the fairest method of deciding, when that which is to be distributed is indivisible. But sometimes welfare considerations can override what is just or fair.

A stock example, in the case of indivisibility, is how to decide which of the two persons shall die because only one kidney is available for transplant. One is young and the other old, and the expected future utility of saving the former's life is much greater than that of saving the latter's life. The only way of treating them with equal respect, of giving them equal chances of living for a while, is to toss a coin. We argue, as we have with respect to redistributive taxation, that sometimes utilitarian considerations can override justice and fairness.

Like Rawls, Ronald Dworkin has tried to construct a set of principles that centre round the notion of equality and define good government. Equality of what? He disagrees with both utilitarianism and the idea that government should aim at equalizing welfare. This is because people should be allowed to enjoy the returns from economic activities which are their own choice and for which they are responsible—activities such as working hard, saving, and taking risks. Similarly, people should not be compensated for losses or ill-fare for which they are responsible. But, so far as possible, people should not gain from the inheritance of material assets, wealth-enhancing genes, or a good upbringing—advantages for which they are not responsible. And they should be compensated for the inheritance of bad genes, and a bad upbringing. Dworkin sums this up by maintaining that it is resources that should be equalized.

There are grave problems with Dworkin's thesis. One cannot equalize abilities for they are not transferable. One can only remove or reduce the returns from ability, and compensate others for lack of ability. But this should be done only in the case of abilities, or the lack of them, for which people have no responsibility. However, it is often very difficult and contentious to assign responsibility. Another problem is that Dworkin gives no criterion of equality for non-transferable resources. In compensating someone for his disability how does one know when one has done enough? The only answer I can think of is when welfare is equalized, or when further compensation would fail to increase the welfare of the disabled. But this would bring Dworkin back to the very thesis he is attacking. Finally, he fails to resolve the obvious contradiction between allowing people the fruits of activities for which they are responsible, and disallowing the development of inequalities of material wealth (he is vehemently against the view that equality of opportunity is a sufficient aim).

We do not believe that equalizing resources provides a better answer than does utilitarianism to the many problems raised by equality (of anything)—problems such as justice, desert, incentives, and the fact that people differ greatly in their ability to transform resources into welfare. Finally, we explain in this chapter the difficulties, which Dworkin ignores, of measuring equality (of anything).

In Chapter 7 we turn to some recent theories which are called contractual, although they bear little resemblence to the theory that the legitimacy and functions of the state spring from a contract. They are deeper in that morality itself is held to derive from the implicit agreements and conventions without which a thriving society is unthinkable. The formation (or failure to form) agreements and conventions on the part of rational individuals is the subject of game theory and the recent contractualists have been much influenced by it.

Implicit agreements, customs, and conventions, have a long history and can, at least partly, be explained in evolutionary terms. Those that are agreed by nearly all rational well-informed people, and are regarded as important for a secure and thriving life, acquire moral force. This means that people come to believe that they ought to obey them. This goes a long way to explaining morality, but does not justify it. However, some contractarians believe that if it can be shown that certain rules must be agreed by rational persons seeking to profit by a cooperative enterprise, then such rules are just. This is what is meant by 'morality by agreement'. Society is a cooperative, coordinating enterprise, and morality constitutes a just division of the gains from cooperation. A basic objection to this moral theory is that rational solutions to problems of coordination do not always exist.

Not all social customs and conventions can be described as implicit agreements about how to divide the gains from cooperation. For instance, a ban on homicide cannot be plausibly described in this way although it is a convention of social behaviour which people believe they ought to obey. Much morality escapes inclusion in the idea of morality by agreement. Morality by convention seems more inclusive. A convention is a rule of behaviour such that almost everyone conforms, and prefers to conform provided almost everyone else conforms, which they all expect. Conventions need not be enforced by any institutionalized authority and are effectively self-enforcing. They are discussed more fully in Chapter 9.

As we have seen, some conventions acquire moral force. But conventions that spring from coordinating actions are not plausibly related to all areas of morality, such as one's duty to one's children or parents. Finally, the theory of morality by convention does not seek to justify all the moral conventions that have developed. Some may be obnoxious, and they can change. One is free to attack the moral codes of any society, including one's own. Chapter 8 on communitarianism concludes Part II. It is too brief to summarize. We hold to the view that the good of communities and nations is reducible to that of individuals.

We proceed to Part III. The overlap of politics and economics is very extensive, and we explore only a small part of the area. In particular we ignore the macroeconomic problem of how best to promote stability and growth. This is a vast subject which requires much more economic expertise and experience than do the other subjects addressed in this book. There is little disagreement about the role of government, and philosophers and politicians would have little to contribute to a discussion of the best means of achieving macroeconomic ends. We concentrate on the provision of public goods and on political economy explanations of policies and trends, together with some reference to the political malfunction of rent-seeking and corruption. We hope that this adequately excuses our neglect of macroeconomics.

Chapter 9 provides a simple introduction to the fringes of game theory. This is needed because game theory is important for exploring whether the economic behaviour of a small number of persons can be satisfactorily coordinated without the intervention of some authority. Conventions are means of achieving a satisfactory equilibrium, or procedure for regulating behaviour, even when the number of people involved is indefinitely large. They are supposed to be self-policing and need no authority. They undoubtedly play a major part in regulating behaviour in all societies. The classic example is driving on the same side of the road.

Pure public goods are classically defined by two characteristics. First, they are in joint supply: this means that their consumption by one person does not preclude simultaneous consumption of the same item by others.[1] Second, and more crucially, they are non-excludable: this means that if the good is produced no one can be excluded from benefiting from it. The classic examples are lighthouses and national defence. Private attempts to produce public goods have to overcome the problem of free-riders, those who enjoy the good without contributing to its cost. There are examples of private provision, and game theory helps to analyse the probability of such provision in different circumstances. The smaller the number of potential beneficiaries, the more likely it is.

Many of the goods that are publicly produced are not public goods. They include health, education, and pensions. They are publicly produced and then given away, or heavily subsidized, for reasons of welfare or equality. But it is questionable whether public *production* is needed to achieve such social ends.

We turn to Chapter 10. For too long economists thought of governments as impartial maximizers of the wealth or welfare of the nation, somehow defined. It was only in the late 1950s that the idea was introduced that governments had their own preferences which must be allowed for in any analysis of economic equilibrium or change. This is known as 'endogenizing government'. The simplest hypothesis is that governments maximize the probability of being re-elected. This is too simple, if only because governments do not always allow elections, but it is important in bringing an analysis of voting to the fore.

There are many paradoxes of voting. Perhaps the two most important are (1) that voting is a bad or impossible way of distributing wealth, and (2) that in national elections a rational citizen does not vote, for his chance of affecting the result is virtually nil, and it is certainly not worthwhile informing himself about the issues. The fact that many people do vote (albeit less than half in some important elections) has not been satisfactorily explained. Other theories such as that of the median voter and the tyranny of the majority, are considered.

We next turn to attempts to explain policies and trends as the outcome of interaction between rational self-interested governments and similar individuals. This is what we term positive political

---

[1] 'Joint supply' is commonly used for this condition in the literature, but unfortunately the phrase has long been used in another sense—there is joint supply when a ewe produces wool and milk in fixed proportions. The phrases 'non-rivalness' or 'non-exclusiveness' of consumption are better.

economy, since it is concerned with how governments behave, and not how they should behave. In the case of more industrialized countries we look at attempts to explain protection, and the growth of government in the past half century. We do not find these attempts at all convincing. Probably, the main reason is the difficulty in modelling government, which is not a unitary institution with well-defined ends as theory tends to require: but what determines voters' opinions on issues affecting economic policy is also very speculative. In the developing world we consider the doctrine of import substitution which dominated economic policy in almost all developing countries for about 30 years. It was largely a case of madmen in authority distilling their frenzy from some academic scribbler of a few years back, to use Keynes's memorable description of much economic policy making. Policy reform in the third world, that is, attempts to return to more beneficial policies, has recently been much studied with a view to discovering the political and economic conditions most conducive to success. The results have been worthwhile, if not very surprising. But we do not find that the ideas of the new political economy have contributed much.

In Chapter 11 we look at some contributions in the areas of politics and economics which have a clear bearing on the central issue of how much government there should be. In Chapter 10 we noted that the distribution of wealth cannot be determined by voting. It follows that if distribution is determined politically, it cannot be determined democratically. How then should it be determined in a democracy?

There is no principle of morality or justice why any one group of persons should earn more or less than another (after allowing for relative disutilities of the work). Redistribution from rich to poor is all right because the rich and the poor do not constitute economic groups. But if government gets into the business of determining the income of different occupations it has no guiding principle, and the result will be determined by the strength of different interest groups in a manner that may be disorderly, and is certainly not democratic. The conclusion is that the government should, as far as possible, steer clear of allocating incomes. This should be left to the market. However, if markets are not competitive then some groups may be able to influence significantly their own incomes which is not morally or politically acceptable. It follows that it is an important function of a democratic government to enforce competition, and discourage all forms of monopoly, including trade unions and employers' and professional associations. The last named have monoploy power, but also the function of protecting consumers against incompetent practice. This complicates any regulation of their activities.

Mancur Olson has analysed the formation and influence of 'distributive coalitions', that is groups whose main purpose is to protect and increase their share of the national income. Such groups are slow to form because of the free-rider problem. But gradually they do form, and exercise a baleful influence on the growth of output, because of their protective, conservative interests, and slowness to take decisions. War and revolution break up these coalitions, and this may account for the superior post-war performance of Germany, Japan, Korea, and Taiwan. I believe this argument has some strength, although I guess that it may be dismissed by some economic historians.

We finally turn in Chapter 11 to the problem of rent-seeking and corruption. Rent-seeking is the expenditure of resources to change economic policy and its impact on particular firms or distributive coalitions. It need not involve corruption though it usually does. Some rent-seeking is unavoidable. But the greater the extent to which governments determine the allocation of wealth, the greater is the practice of rent-seeking and corruption. It is a very serious problem, which can grow to pervade the political system. Democracy is then likely to break down and often has.

Of course, not all publicity and lobbying is rent-seeking. Some is directed towards socially desirable causes. It is a means, however imperfect, of influencing government, which must be permitted in a democracy. But sometimes there may be an element of rent-seeking in the promotion of a good cause. Conceptually, the distinction between rent-seeking and unselfish promotion is clear, but in practice which side of the boundary some activity mainly falls will often be debatable.

THE PHILOSOPHICAL FRAMEWORK

Discussion of many of the problems considered in Parts I to III can be closed only with a value judgement. In some cases I have not effected any closure, and have remained sitting on the fence. However, a definite position has sometimes been taken, which may have seemed arbitrary. Further explanation is warranted.

My general position is anti-metaphysical. I do not believe that there are recognizable moral characteristics, such as goodness or rightness. I do not believe that any moral injunction can be shown to follow from pure reason. In particular, I do not accept Kant's categorical imperative.

The language of ethics has a different structure and different rules to that of descriptive or predictive discourse. Ethical statements are intended to influence people's behaviour. They are closer to imperatives than to factual statements. However, some value judgements have both descriptive and evaluative content. If I say 'Robert is a cruel boy', I am implying both that he does something like pulling wings off flies, and that one should not behave like that. This does not invalidate an essential distinction. If I am told both to go, and to stay, these are contradictory instructions, but 'go' and 'stay' are not contradictions in the same sense as 'A is B' and 'A is not B'. The latter propositions have conflicting truth values. If A is B, then 'A is B' is true, and 'A is not B' is false. But 'go' and 'stay' do not have truth values. However, there may be no generally accepted and precise criterion as to whether some proposition is true or false, in which case people may disagree in good faith. When this is the case, then the proposition must be treated as a value judgement, with no clear truth values. Most of the propositions of welfare economics are of this type. Welfare economics, as the very term 'welfare' implies, is a branch of applied ethics.

Why do people make moral judgements? Why do they tell others what they ought to do or what is right? It is clear that people living together in society need to be able to rely on other people behaving in certain ways. They need to be safe from attack, and to be able to own things which others may not take from them, and to be able to make promises and to trust others to keep their promises; they need rules to help them avoid conflict and resolve differences of interest, and so on; and so on. We have seen that conventions and customs grow in every society to facilitate social interaction. These very probably have an evolutionary explanation, but that is not essential for our argument. What is essential is that many of these conventions come to have moral force which means that people come to believe that they ought to obey them. I believe this is the source of all moral codes. I argued earlier that some duties, for instance, duties to one's children, cannot plausibly be regarded as springing from any convention regulating social interaction. But we can finesse this objection, by arguing that the habits which define good parenting (and other familial duties) have evolutionary value, and that such habits or customs can, like conventions, acquire moral force. With this proviso, I argue that all moral rules spring from custom and convention. Obviously, I do not expect theists to agree.

However, this does not exhaust the subject of morality. Rules need interpretation. It is not always clear whether or not a certain rule applies in a particular situation, and often a decision needs to be taken when no rule seems to apply. If this were not the case we would not have moral disagreements. In this book I have occasionally rejected a proposition because most people would not agree with it, for instance that the state has no right to redistribute property. But this should not be interpreted as implying that consensus is a determining factor in any moral argument.

We need to discuss the genesis of right. People create and acquire rights as part of the process of socialization. It is a convention that promises create both duties and rights. That promises should be kept is a convention that has acquired moral force as already described. In our view the state acquires and creates duties and rights in the same way, that is conventionally. By now, after about 100 years, many states have acquired a right to enact redistributive taxation: this has become part of the moral ethos that regulates society. Codes do change, albeit slowly. However, at this point, I must insist that any person is free to disagree with any part of the moral code or ethos of his or any other society.

Where does all this leave utilitarianism, a doctrine to which we have devoted many pages of this book? Utilitarianism is a version of consequentialism, which holds that whether some action is right or wrong depends solely on its consequences. Utililitarianism further holds that the only consequences that count are the well-beings of persons. We do not subscribe to this view for we admit that there are some things which one must not do to anyone—murder them, torture them, or imprison them knowing that they are innocent—and that this overrides considerations of welfare. But admitting such side constraints does not render utilitarianism useless—far from it. It may still be thought of as a guide to behaviour in many situations.

How do we reconcile utilitarianism with the moral codes that consist of numerous rules and conventions which people believe they ought to obey? We have just claimed that there are some moral rules which are so strong that they override welfare considerations. But most rules are not absolute guides that brook no exception.

Telling lies is an obvious example. Sometimes one considers good consequences that may come from telling a lie, and weighs them against the bad consequences of breaking a moral rule in which one believes (breaking the rule is itself bad, and this can be counted among the consequences). Such thinking is essentially utilitarian.

Utilitarianism may not be a very useful guide for the individual. Certainly, few individuals will accept one of the traditional tenets of the doctrine—that everyone should count for one. Almost everyone puts more weight on the welfare of his family, his friends, and indeed his cat and his dog, than he does on strangers. Assessing the consequences of breaking a moral rule may then become so complicated as to seem implausible. Probably many people go through life obeying rules, and disobeying them, only by some instinct which is unanalysable. But I think many people also employ the utilitarian calculus, especially in situations where no rule seems to apply.

We believe that utilitarianism is a much better guide for state or governmental behaviour than for individuals. A moral proposition, which is at least as widely acclaimed as any other, is that governments should be, so far as possible, impartial: that is, everyone's utility should have the same weight. But the basic function of government is to protect persons and their property, and enforce contracts and the rule of law. Utilitarianism comes in only with acceptance of the view that governments should go further, and interfere with the results of private activity.

It is commonly argued that governments should step in when there are failures of the price mechanism: or, more generally, when private interaction fails to produce the best results, which may be called market failure. This covers—at least in part—the production of public goods, externalities, and monopolistic behaviour. But how is failure determined? By what standard is an outcome deemed inferior? It has to be by appeal to some function of the utilities of individuals—that is, some form of utilitarianism. And when government has in fact become responsible for the production of some good, how does it decide how much currently to produce, what investments to make, and so on? The economists' answer is by cost-benefit analysis, which is utilitarian. The main alternative has been the whim of some politician or powerful bureaucrat with a bee in his bonnet about appropriate products or modes of production—or with a palm outstretched for the kickback.

There are two further commonly accepted grounds for government intervention, redistribution (that is, equality), and paternalism.

We have considered attempts to make equality the goal which should determine intervention (and the design of all authoritative institutions). Equality of what? Not welfare—shades of utilitarianism!—but resources or basic goods. We have dismissed these theories as clearly inferior to utilitarianism.

There remains paternalism: that is interfering with people's free choices on grounds other than that they have external effects on other people. It is presumed that people's choices as affected by prohibitions, and by taxation or subsidization, are a better measure of their own welfare than their unaffected choices. On what principles is it decided that education should be compulsory, and up to what age; that cigarettes should be heavily taxed; that cannabis should or should not be illegal; that opera should be subsidized? I find it difficult to think of a guiding light other than utilitarianism to illuminate such varied problems where externalities, even if they exist, are a minor matter. It may be admitted that utilitarianism itself is a feeble flickering light in some cases, especially perhaps when it comes to intervention in artistic and cultural matters.

Some contractarians, for instance Binmore and Scanlon, admit that utilitarianism has a role. It has been remarked that we would want a benevolent dictator to be a utilitarian. (What else?) But we do not want a dictator: his benevolence, if it ever existed, does not last. The function of democracy is to prevent dictatorship. It has serious flaws as a decision-making procedure, and can lead to many outcomes that are sub-optimal by utilitarian criteria. But it may on balance enhance welfare by making dictatorship, with all the hideous evils that it has caused in the twentieth century, more difficult to achieve.

THE SCALE OF GOVERNMENT EXPENDITURE

How much should be spent on goods and services that the government provides free, or virtually free, at the point of use? There is no good way of deciding, because there is no market. If there were a perfect market, the amount provided would be the right amount (we abstract from consumption externalities and paternalistic considerations). When it can be shown that the market is imperfect, then there will be good reasons for judging that what is provided is too much or too little. The market provides a basis for judging. But in the case of pure public goods, and those supplied free for welfare or ideological reasons, there is no market.

Ethics, Economics, and Politics

Can it nevertheless be shown that too much or too little is pro-vided? There may be queuing, or other forms of rationing. This shows that there is excess demand when the price is zero, but not that people would be willing to pay enough to cover the cost of what they are getting. It does not show that too little is provided, though that may be the case. Occasionally there is excess supply even when the service is free; an example would be a museum that could handle more visitors without more staff. Nothing follows; for the few visitors might have been willing to pay enough to main-tain the museum. If free university education is provided, and places are fully taken up, that does not indicate that some students would not have been better-off without it. In the case of national defence, expenditure is a poor indicator of whether there is an ade-quate deterrent, or who will win the next war.

Where there is no market, provision has to be made politically. Enough has been said to show that political decision-making is highly imperfect. It is one of the theses of the public-choice school of Buchanan and others that bureaucratic failure may be worse than market failure.

Voting, as we have seen, is a poor way of deciding many issues. In practice, particular projects and policies with their consequential expenditures are rarely decided by voting. At the national level, voters normally only choose parties to form governments, and parties have vague platforms covering a wide range of issues. One of the parties may be more in favour of big government and high taxation than another. This may or may not be decisive as to which is elected for a term: but it does not decide how much is spent on different goods and services. Occasionally, a party may correctly sense that the electorate is especially concerned about a particular service, and there may then be some voter influence on how much is spent. This does not mean that the influence is good. As we have seen, popu-larity is a poor indicator of economic value. However, lobbying by special interests, and distributive coalitions, are frequently more important than individual voters. But there is equally little reason to suppose that the strength of a lobby is closely connected with the social value of its objectives.

There are several reasons for suspecting a bias in favour of high public spending. The median voter may feel more in need of good public service than he fears that rising taxes will hurt him. Governments often hand out subsidies or tax cuts before an election. A senior bureaucrat's pay normally rises with the number of employees in his department. Similarly, the minister's prestige and influence, and maybe his pay, is greater the larger is his ministry. He will almost always be arguing in favour of more spending. Where corruption is very serious, which is true of almost all third-world and ex-Soviet Union countries, it goes hand-in-hand with the extent of government spending and regulation. However, such reasons do not decisively lead to excessive spending. Corruption and political vote buying may result in a public service being starved of revenue, with consequent underinvestment. This has notoriously resulted in serious underinvestment in infrastructural services in India and other developing countries. It has been argued that privatization is sometimes needed to ensure sufficient investment.

Public expenditure includes subsidies to public industries where there is a market for the product but losses are made. It is widely believed, and there is good evidence for it, that public production is usually relatively inefficient—the basic reason being that incentives to minimize costs in the public sector are inadequate. To the extent that public production makes losses, and is therefore subsidized, privatization reduces public expenditure.

The argument thus far implies that production should not be in the public sector, unless there are welfare objectives which can only be adequately met by public production. In the UK, privatization has gone a long way since 1980, and industrial subsidies have been greatly reduced. Public expenditure on housing has also been greatly reduced, though this is at least partly offset by a rise in housing benefit.

Any discussion therefore of whether there is too much or too little government expenditure (in the UK) has to concentrate on the two sectors still dominated by public production, health and education, which together comprise over a quarter of total government expenditure. Social security transfer payments account for another third or more (the two together comprise about 60 per cent).[2] These transfers differ in that they do not involve public production. In all three areas the welfare and efficiency arguments are complex, and

[2] See Andrew Tyrie (1996), Table 1. This is a very useful survey of the subject. The figures quoted are for 1995–96. I apologise for the UK-centricity of the following pages: but I think the arguments have wide validity. See also Flemming and Oppenheimer (1996).

little can be said with much confidence without deep study which would take one far beyond the confines of a short introductory book. We can give only a sketch of the issues involved.

We have argued against public production unless it can (unusually) be shown to be as efficient as private production, and unless certain welfare objectives are unattainable without public production. So we should ask the most basic question—cannot all welfare needs be reached by income support of the very poor and incapacitated, leaving people free to choose how much health and education they want? Even if the answer were 'Yes', it must be noted that the outcome would not necessarily be very efficient. Well-targeted benefits need a lot of expert administration, and also have psychological costs. And safety nets produce poverty and savings traps. Why work if one earns little more than the loss of benefit? Why save if this only reduces a means-tested state pension? These are not conclusive arguments but they need to be considered.

In the case of health, it is clearly possible to reconcile private production with welfare objectives. The UK is one of the very few countries with a comprehensive National Health Service. Yet the poor and incapacitated are, we believe, well looked after at least in the wealthier European countries. However, the UK's expenditure on health as a percentage of GDP is much lower than in most European countries—a little over six per cent as against a European Union average of eight per cent. But it is also true that some life expectancy, and infant mortality, rates are worse than the European average, and complaints of poor hospital service are rife. It seems that the National Health Service (NHS) is relatively cost-effective, but absolute standards are not always acceptable. Despite this, only a small minority of the population would like to see the end of the NHS. This does not add up to a strong case for very extensive privatization, although more use of, and better integration with, the private sector may well be possible.[3] The present government's intention is to raise the percentage of national income spent on the Health Service.

Education is different in that there has always been a strong paternalistic element. Parents could not be trusted to spend enough on education. When it became compulsory it also had to be free. However, compulsion can be combined with private schools

---

[3] See *Securing Our Future Health*, The Stationery Office, 2001.

by giving education tokens to parents, that is money that can be spent only on schooling. The value of the tokens could be the same for all families with the same profile of children, or could vary negatively with, say, income tax paid. Parents could then have a choice of schools, which would be able to compete not only in the token cost, but also in the content and style of the education offered. This is an attractive idea if only because UK children do not fare well in international comparisons, but also because there is a widespread perception that standards have recently fallen (whatever exam results claim). This is less a matter of reducing expenditure than improving the quality of education. A reduction in the influence of the Ministry might improve matters, though no doubt some public inspection of schools would be maintained. Some may feel it is unseemly that a school should be run for profit. In my opinion this is an outdated prejudice; after all the suppliers of our daily bread work for profit. It is also the case that many private schools are owned by trustees, and are not run for profit.

Finally, we consider social security expenditures. Apart from pensions these consist of (1) payments to those who lose earnings because of illness or disability; (2) a variety of family support schemes; and (3) unemployment and housing benefit. These expenditures do not involve production. There is no criterion as to how generous the government should be. Somehow or other it gets decided with benevolent lobbyists on one side, and the politicians who fear raising taxes on the other. It is well-known that cheating is widespread and may be measured in £ billions. But it is very hard for administrators to be both caring, and tough on fraud.

This leaves pensions, a subject on which economists have a lot to say. In the UK there is no production in the public sector (apart from administration). Public pensions are not produced through the investment of funds; they are simply another transfer, essentially from earners to the retired. They account, in the UK, for about half of all social security spending.

There is a lot to be said in favour of funded pensions: the amount of the pension is then determined by the amount contributed. This is more transparent for the subscriber who can observe his fund growing, and the probable income it will produce. It also ensures against dangerous over-provision of pensions, with a smaller cohort of workers paying the pensions of an ever-increasing number of retirees. In principle, state pensions could be funded, and probably should be. There is a problem of transition from one system to the other, but I believe it could be overcome.

There are, of course, many private funded pension schemes. Is there any reason for state pensions at all: or for all the paraphernalia of schemes for reducing the taxation of savings? These latter exist only because the income-tax system double-taxes savings— savings are made from taxed income, and then the proceeds of the savings are taxed again as income. This makes it clear that it is difficult to consider pensions without a basic review of the whole tax system, including expenditure and wealth taxes that do not double-tax savings.

For the sake of argument, assume that only expenditure is taxed, so that savings are made tax free. People would be free to save and invest as they choose; and pension schemes, which exist only to take advantage of the reliefs from double taxation that the government gives, would vanish. What in these circumstances would be the rationale of a state pension? It would be there only as a means-tested safety net—indeed it would be indistinguishable in principle from other income supports. Admittedly, there would then be a savings trap. If the state pension was £5,000 per annum, it might take savings of, say, £60,000 to buy an equivalent annuity on retirement at the age of 65. If this were fully subtracted from one's state pension entitlement, then the first £60,000 of savings would in effect be a gift to the government. I do not think this is a compelling argument against a means-tested pension any more than the poverty trap is a compelling argument against income support. At the worst no one would save, and the (unfunded) state pension would be fully used. But I do not think this very likely. At present, the tax system makes saving a very unattractive option without the various reliefs obtainable. If savings were not taxed at all, the incentive to save would be greatly increased. People would save. Enough has been said to show that this is a very complicated subject, but one where the possibilities of beneficial reform are large.

Minimum government enthusiasts will be disappointed by this section. So long as welfare is accepted as a responsibility of government, there has to be a good deal of government. But production in the public sector is usually both inefficient and unneccessary (we except the NHS in the UK). We also believe that it should be minimized on the ground that the less government is responsible for the relative earnings in different occupations or sectors the better. Since there is no principle governing relative earnings their politicization is a dangerous source of conflict. This also applies to the tax and subsidy treatment, and the regulation, of different activities. So far as possible, pre-tax incomes should be settled by the market. However, this makes it imperative that the government should act forcefully against the formation of 'distributive coalitions', and in general promote competition. Where such coalitions have useful social functions, they must be supervised or the functions be taken over by government. I believe that considerable gains in efficiency and welfare are possible, but that the principles adumbrated would not result in very much reduction of government expenditure. This goes for the UK, but not everywhere. For instance, I believe that a large reduction of government would be highly beneficial in India.

THE BOUNDARIES OF PUBLIC POLICY

In our discussion of the scale of government expenditure we have roughly marked out the boundaries of public policy. The government should ensure law and order; deal with failures of the price mechanism, including where needed the provision of public goods, the correction of externalities, and the control or discouragement of monopoly. It should also be responsible for eliminating severe poverty, to the extent possible, using redistributive taxation and other measures. It should rarely indulge in public sector production (but we excepted the UK's NHS largely because it exists and people have become accustomed to it).

The argument that the government should be responsible for the very poor raises the question of what else, if anything, we should want the government to take responsibility for. This is another way of approaching the question of the boundaries of public policy. For many years after 1945 the UK government accepted responsibility for full employment. This was abandoned when it became apparent that it was an obligation it could not fulfil. Governments have sometimes unwisely come close to promising a certain rate of economic growth. More recently, a low rate of inflation has come to be regarded as a responsibility of government. Since this is almost synonymous with the provision of a sound currency, it can be properly regarded as a public good, and therefore clearly a responsibility of government.

The public production of other services, in particular health and education, makes it difficult not to have targets and standards, which the government becomes responsible for, although there is no objective criterion of what these targets should be and how much should be spent on getting good scores. This may be regarded as yet another argument against the public production of goods or services. Admittedly, we found that there was no strong case for privatization of the UK's NHS. But the main argument for keeping it despite its failings was popular support. However, we are not aware that there is any strong demand for a NHS where none exists, for instance in the USA or some continental European countries. Similar considerations apply to education, but less so partly because governments do not usually produce higher education, and partly because a person has the final say as to how much education he or she will absorb. Sometimes the government gets involved in an issue, such as savings and pensions, as an unwanted by-product of its other activities which are financed by taxation that unduly discourages saving. This should be classified as bureaucratic failure, and the remedy lies with tax reform. The mention of savings raises the question of the responsibility of government for ameliorating not only present poverty but also for future poverty: or, since future governments can look after the future poor, for the general wealth of future generations. I do not think that one can deny that future people are part of the government's constituency (although one might want the government to put a low weight on the utility of people as yet unborn). But their wealth will depend on their numbers as well as on current savings. One can hardly suggest that a government should have a savings target without a population target, and vice versa. I think a case can be made for population and savings targets only in some developing countries where the rate of growth of population is very high—say, over two per cent per annum. At least the possible effect of other policies on births and savings should be a consideration. However, any direct constraint on a person's freedom to choose to have children is probably unacceptable in most cultures, although expenditure on information, persuasion, and even subsidization of contraception, is now commonly acceptable.

This brings us finally to the question of whether there is ever any good reason to interfere with individual choices provided they do not affect other persons' welfare. Interference on clearly religious or doctrinal grounds is anathema to this author. But should the government try to change people's behaviour for their own good, either by legal restriction or by using taxes and subsidies? I think not. But such an opinion may seldom be decisive, for very often it can be argued in favour of some prohibition, or subsidization of 'merit' goods, that other people are or will be adversely or favourably affected: and this is very difficult to prove or disprove. Moreover, some degree of external harm or benefit does not necessarily outweigh the denial of personal freedom of choice. Paternalism always presents a dilemma because it essentially involves a conflict of values, freedom versus welfare. There is no general way of resolving this. Pluralism must reign, and every case needs special consideration.

References

Ahluwalia, I. and I.M.D. Little (eds) (1998) *India's Economic Reforms and Development*, Oxford University Press, Delhi.

Aristotle (c.330 BC) *Nicomachean Ethics*.

Arrow, K. (1951) *Social Choice and Individual Values*, Yale University Press.

—— and G. Debreu (1954) 'Existence of an Equilibrium for a Competitive Economy', *Econometrica*, 22.

—— and T. Scitovsky (eds) (1969) *Readings in Welfare Economics*, R.D. Irwin.

Atkinson, A.B. (1970) 'On the Measurement of Inequality', *Journal of Economic Theory*, 2.

Baier, K. (1958) *The Moral Point of View: A Rational Basis of Ethics*, Ithaca, New York.

Balch, M.S., D. McFadden, and S.Y. Wu (eds) (1974) *Economic Behaviour and Uncertainty*, North Holland.

Barry, B. (1973) *The Liberal Theory of Justice*, Clarendon Press, Oxford.

—— (1995) *Justice as Impartiality*, Clarendon Press, Oxford.

—— and R. Hardin (eds) (1982) *Rational Man and Irrational Society*, Sage Publications.

Bates, R.H., S. Haggard and J. Nelson (1991) 'A Critique of Political Scientists' in Meier (ed.) (1991).

Berlin, I. (1969) 'Two Concepts of Liberty' in *Four Essays on Liberty*, Oxford University Press.

Besley, T. and Anne Case (1995) 'Does Electoral Accountability Affect Economic Policy Choices? Evidence from Gubernatorial Term Limits', *Quarterly Journal of Economics*, 110(3).

Bhagwati, J. (1979) *Anatomy and Consequences of Trade Control Regimes*, NBER and Ballinger.

—— (1982) 'The Welfare Consequences of Directly Unproductive Profit-Seeking (DUP) Lobbying Activities', *Journal of International Economics*, 13.

—— (1990) 'The Theory of Political Economy, Economic Policy, and Foreign Investment' in Scott, M. and D. Lal (eds) (1990).

Binmore, K. (1993) 'Bargaining and Morality' in Gauthier and Sugden (eds).

—— (1994 and 1998) *Game Theory and the Social Contract*, Vol. 1, *Playing Fair*; Vol. 2, *Just Playing*, MIT Press.

Black, D. (1948) 'On the Rationale of Group Decision Making', *Journal of Political Economy*, 56, reprinted in Arrow and Scitovsky (eds) (1969).

—— (1958) *The Theory of Committees and Elections*, Cambridge University Press.

Blackorby, C. and Donaldson, D. (1984) 'Social Criteria for Evaluating Population Change', *Journal of Public Economics*, 25.

Boskin, M.J. (ed.) (1979) *Economics and Human Welfare*, Academic Press.

Broome, J. (1991) *Weighing Goods*, Blackwell.

—— (1992) *Counting the Cost of Global Warming*, The White Horse Press.

—— (1999) *Ethics out of Economics*, Cambridge University Press.

Buchanan, J. (1954) 'Social Choice, Democracy, and Free Markets', *Journal of Political Economy*, LXII.

—— and G. Tullock (1962) *The Calculus of Consent*, University of Michigan Press.

Clark, J. (1885) *The Philosophy of Wealth*.

Coase, R. (1960) 'The Problem of Social Cost', *Journal of Law and Economics*, 3.

Daniels, N. (ed) (1975) *Reading Rawls*, Blackwell.

Demsetz, H. (1967) 'Towards a Theory of Property Rights', *American Economic Review*, 57.

Downs, A. (1957) *An Economic Theory of Democracy*, Harper & Row.

Drazen, A. (2000) *Political Economy in Macroeconomics*, Princeton University Press.

Dworkin, R. (1978) *Taking Rights Seriously*, Duckworth.

—— (2000) *Sovereign Virtue, the Theory and Practice of Equality*, Harvard University Press.

Farina, F., F. Hahn, and S. Vanucci (eds) (1996) *Ethics, Rationality, and Economic Behaviour*, Clarendon Press, Oxford.

Flemming, J. and P. Oppenheimer (1996) 'Are Government Spending and Taxes Too High (or Too Low)?', *National Institute Economic Review*, July.

Gauthier, D. (1986) *Morals by Agreement*, Clarendon Press, Oxford.

—— and R. Sugden (eds) (1993) *Rationality, Justice and the Social Contract*, Harvester Wheatsheaf.

Giersch, H. (ed.) (1987) *Free Trade in the World Economy*, J.C.B. Mohr.

Graaff, J. de V. (1962) 'On Making a Recommendation in a Democracy', *Economic Journal*, LXXII, reprinted in Rowley (ed.) (1993).

Green, D. and I. Shapiro (1994) *Pathologies of Rational Choice Theory*, Yale University Press.

Grice, G.R. (1967) *The Grounds of Moral Judgement*, Cambridge University Press.

Grossman, G. and K. Rogoff (eds) (1995) *Handbook of International Economics*, Vol. 3, North Holland.

Haggard, S. and R. Kaufman (eds) (1992) *The Politics of Economic Adjustment*, Princeton University Press.

Hammond, P. (1982) 'Utilitarianism, uncertainty and information' in Sen and Williams (eds).

Hampton, J. (1987) 'Free-Rider Problems in the Production of Collective Goods', *Economics and Philosophy*, 3.

Hare, R.M. (1952) *The Language of Morals*, Clarendon Press, Oxford.

—— (1981) *Moral Thinking*, Clarendon Press, Oxford.

Hare, R.M. (1989) *Essays in Moral Theory*, Oxford University Press.

Harsanyi, J.C. (1953) 'Cardinal utility in welfare economics and in the theory of risk taking', *Journal of Political Economy*, 61, reprinted in Harsanyi (1976).

—— (1955) 'Cardinal Welfare, Individualistic Ethics, and Interpersonal Comparisons of Utility', *Journal of Political Economy*, 69, reprinted in Harsanyi (1976).

—— (1976) *Essays on Ethics, Social Behavior and Scientific Explanation*, Reidel.

—— (1996) 'Morality and Incentives' in Farina, Hahn and Venucci (eds).

Hart, H.L.A. (1955) 'Are there any natural rights?', *Philosophical Review*, 64, reprinted in Quinton (ed.).

Hobbes, T. (1651) *Leviathan*.

Hotelling, H. (1929) 'Stability and Competition', *Economic Journal*, 39.

Hume, D. (1740) *A Treatise of Human Nature*, Book III, Part II, sections ii–v.

—— (1751) *An Enquiry Concerning the Principles of Morals*.

Hutcheson, F. (1755) *A System of Moral Philosophy*.

Jasay, A. de (1985) *The State*, Blackwell.

—— (1989) *Social Contract, Free Ride*, Clarendon Press, Oxford.

—— (1998) 'Justice' in *The New Palgrave Dictionary of Economics and the Law*, Macmillan.

—— (1998) 'Prisoners' dilemma and the theory of the state' in *The New Palgrave Dictionary of Economics and the Law*, Macmillan.

Joshi, Mary S., Vijay Joshi, and Roger Lamb (2001) 'City Centre Traffic and the Prisoner's Dilemma', University of Oxford, Department of Economics Discussion Paper Series, No 85.

Joshi, V. and I.M.D. Little (1997) *India's Economic Reforms*, Oxford University Press.

Kant, I. (republished 1964) *Groundwork of the Metaphysic of Morals*, trans H. Paton, Harper Torchbooks, New York.

Krueger, A. (1974) 'The Political Economy of the Rent-seeking Society', *American Economic Review*, 64, No 3.

—— (1978) *Liberalization Attempts and Consequences*, NBER and Ballinger.

—— (1990) 'The Political Economy of Controls: American Sugar' in Scott and Lal (eds).

—— (1993) *Political Economy of Policy Reform in Developing Countries*, MIT Press.

—— (ed.) (2000) *Economic Policy Reform*, University of Chicago Press.

Kymlicka, W. (1990) *Contemporary Political Philosophy*, Clarendon Press, Oxford.

Lal, D. and H. Myint (1996) *The Political Economy of Poverty, Equity and Growth*, Clarendon Press, Oxford.

Lane, R.E. (2000) *The Loss of Happiness in Market Democracies*, Yale University Press.

Lewis, D. (1965) *Conventions—a Philosophical Study*, Harvard University Press.

Little, I.M.D. (1957) *A Critique of Welfare Economics* (second edn), Clarendon Press, Oxford.

—— (1979) 'Welfare Criteria, Distribution and Cost-Benefit Analysis' in Boskin (ed.).

—— (1980) 'Distributive Justice and the New International Order' in Oppenheimer (ed.), reprinted in Little (1999).

—— (1999) *Collection and Recollections*, Clarendon Press, Oxford.

—— and J.A. Mirrlees (1974) *Project Appraisal and Planning for Developing Countries*, Heinemann (reprinted Gower 1988).

Locke, J. (1690) *Two Treatises on Government*.

Lyons, D. (1982) 'The new Indian claims and original rights to land' in Paul (ed.).

MacIntyre, A. (1985) *After Virtue* (second edn), Duckworth.

Magee, S. (1987) 'The Political Economy of US Protection' in Giersch (ed.), (1987).

Meier, G.M. (ed.) (1991) *Politics and Policy Making in Developing Countries*, ICS Press, San Francisco.

Michaely, M., D. Papageorgiou and A. Choksi (1991) *Liberalizing Foreign Trade*, Blackwell.

Mirrlees, J.A. (1974) 'Notes on Welfare Economics, Information and Uncertainty' in Balch, McFadden, and Wu (eds).

—— (1982) 'The Economic Uses of Utilitarianism' in Sen and Williams (eds).

Mueller, D. (1989) *Public Choice II*, Cambridge University Press.

—— (1997) *Perspectives on Public Choice*, Cambridge University Press.

Nelson, J. (ed.) (1990) *Economic Crisis and Policy Choice*, Princeton University Press.

Nozick, R. (1974) *Anarchy, State, and Utopia*, Blackwell.

Offer, A. (2000) 'Economic Welfare Measurements and Human Well Being', *University of Oxford Discussion Papers in Economic and Social History*, 34.

Olson, M. (1965) *The Logic of Collective Action*, Harvard University Press.

—— (1982) *The Rise and Decline of Nations*, Yale University Press.

Oppenheimer, P. (ed.) (1980) *Issues in International Economics*, Oriel Press.

Parfit, D. (1984) *Reasons and Persons*, Clarendon Press, Oxford.

Paul, J. (ed.) (1982) *Reading Nozick, Essays on Anarchy, State and Utopia*, Blackwell.

Persson, T. and G. Tabellini (2000) *Political Economics*, MIT Press.

Pettit, P. (1987) 'Universalisability without Utilitarianism', *Mind*, 96.

Pigou, A.C. (1946) *The Economics of Welfare* (fourth edn), Macmillan.

Poterba, J.M. (1994) 'State Response to Fiscal Crises: The Effects of Budgetary Institutions and Politics', *Journal of Political Economy*, Vol. 102, Issue 4.

Proudhon, P.-J. (1840) *What is Property?*

Quinton, A. (ed.) (1967) *Political Philosophy*, Oxford University Press.

Ramsey, F.P. (1926) 'Truth and Probability' in Ramsey (1931).

—— (1931) *The Foundations of Mathematics*, Kegan Paul.

Rawls, J. (1958) 'Justice as Fairness', *The Philosophical Review*, 57.

—— (1988) 'Classical Utilitarianism' in Scheffler (ed.).

—— (1999) *A Theory of Justice, Revised Edition*, Oxford University Press.

Raz, J. (1986) *The Morality of Freedom*, Clarendon Press, Oxford.

Robbins, L. (1938) 'Interpersonal Comparisons of Utility', *Economic Journal*, 48.

Rodrik, D. (1995) 'Political Economy of Trade Policy' in Grossman and Rogoff (eds).

Roemer, J. (1986) 'Equality of Resources Implies Equality of Welfare', *Quarterly Journal of Economics*, 101.

—— (1996) *Theories of Distributive Justice*.

Rowley, C. (ed.) (1993) *Social Choice Theory*, Edward Elgar.

Samuelson, P.A. (1954) 'The Pure Theory of Public Expenditure', *Review of Economics and Statistics*, 36.

Sandel, M. (1982) *Liberalism and the Limits of Justice*, Cambridge University Press.

Scanlon, T.M. (1982) 'Contractarianism and Utilitarianism' in Sen and Williams (eds).

—— (1998) *What We Owe To Eachother*, Harvard University Press.

Scheffler, S. (1988) *Consequentialism and its Critics*, Oxford University Press.

Schumpeter, J.A. (1954) *History of Economic Analysis*, Oxford University Press, New York.

Scott, M. and D. Lal (eds) (1990) *Public Policy and Economic Development*, Clarendon Press, Oxford.

Sen, A.K. (1973) *On Economic Inequality*, Clarendon Press, Oxford.

—— (1982) *Choice, Welfare and Measurement*, Blackwell.

—— (1984) *Resources, Values and Development*, Harvard University Press.

—— and B. Williams (1982) *Utilitarianism and Beyond*, Cambridge University Press.

Srinivasan, T.N. (1991) 'Foreign Trade Regimes' in Meier (ed.) (1991).

—— (2000) 'Economic Reform in South Asia' in Krueger (ed.) (2000).

Stolper, W. and P.A. Samuelson (1941) 'Protection and Real Wages', *Review of Economic Studies*, 9, no 1.

Sugden, R. (1986) *The Economics of Rights, Co-operation and Welfare*, Blackwell.

—— (1988) 'Conventions' in *The New Palgrave Dictionary of Economics and the Law*, Macmillan.

—— (1991) 'Rational Choice: A Survey of Contributions from Economics and Philosophy', *Economic Journal*, Vol. 101.

—— (1993) 'The Contractarian Enterprise' and 'Rationality and impartiality: Is the contractarian enterprise possible?' in Gauthier and Sugden (eds).

Taylor, C. (1995) *Philosophical Arguments*, Harvard University Press.

Temkin, L. (1993) *Inequality*, Oxford University Press.

Tullock, G. (1962) Appendix 2 in Buchanan and Tullock (1962).

Tyrie, A. (1996) *The Prospects for Public Spending*, Social Market Foundation.

Usher, D. (1981) *The Economic Prerequisite to Democracy*, Blackwell.

Vickrey, W. (1960) 'Utility, Strategy and Social Decision Rules', *Quarterly Journal of Economics*, 74, reprinted in Barry and Hardin (eds) (1982).

von Neumann and O. Morgenstern (1944) *The Theory of Games and Economic Behaviour*, Princeton University Press.

Williamson, J. (1990) *Latin American Adjustment: How Much has Happened?*, Institute for International Economics, Washington.

—— (1994) *Political Economy of Policy Reforms*, Institute for International Economics, Washington.

Index of Names

Index of Subjects